With the
Silent Glimmer
of
God's Spirit

With the Silent Glimmer of God's Spirit

A Postmodern Look at the Sacraments

Lambert J. Leijssen

Translated by Marie Baird

With a Foreword by
George S. Worgul, Jr.

Paulist Press
New York/Mahwah, NJ

Paulist Press acknowledges the assistance of Duquesne University, who provided a grant for the translation of the original text into English.

Cover design by Sharyn Banks
Book design by Lynn Else

Library of Congress Cataloging-in-Publication Data

Leijssen, Lambert.
    With the silent glimmer of God's spirit : a postmodern look at the sacraments / Lambert J. Leijssen ; translated by Marie Baird.
        p.   cm.
    ISBN 0-8091-4437-9 (alk. paper)
    1. Sacraments—Catholic Church. 2. Sacraments. 3. Christianity and culture. I. Title.
BX2200.L45 2007
234′.16—dc22

2006025635

Published by Paulist Press
997 Macarthur Boulevard
Mahwah, New Jersey 07430

www.paulistpress.com

Printed and bound in the
United States of America

CONTENTS

Contents

PREFACE

In this book I invite you to explore with me current sacramental theology. New visions of our topic have been developed in recent years, and we shall pay special attention to the changing philosophical context of postmodernity.

Anthropologists would classify the Christian sacraments among the forms of expression of religious feeling and experience. The sacraments are situated in the ritual sphere of humanity. They are *life rituals*. This is the first domain that we will explore in order to determine precisely the place of the sacraments in the attitude of faith that is experienced simultaneously in personal prayer and ethical engagement. It is peculiar to the sacraments as *signs of faith* to be situated within the Christian worldview that, as tradition and choice, is an answer to God's revelation in Jesus Christ. With that, we land in the domain of theology. A theology of the sacraments must presuppose a fundamental theology about God's revelation, in which the foundations of our faith are examined. Western sacramental theology has developed in close affiliation with Christology. "Sacraments are actions of Christ in and through the Church" has become a classic pronouncement. The title of Edward Schillebeeckx's speculative synthesis on the meaning of the sacraments—*Christ, the Sacrament of the Encounter with God*—bears witness to this. The greatest merit of the Dominican theologian's book lies in its reformulation of sacramental theology within the framework of personalism and existentialism, as a corrective to Thomistic essentialism and thought about causality. In postmodern thought the philosophy of being, ontology, and metaphysics that supports classical theology is nevertheless undergoing deeper scrutiny. A new reformulation is urgently needed.

That is the challenge we will take on. How can the visible presence of Jesus, God's greatest revelation, be furthered in the acts of the church? How is the freeing power of his paschal mystery further emphasized and effectively communicated to the faithful? We believe *that* this happens in the sacraments. The theological task is reflexively to ascertain and clarify in an acceptable way *how* that happens. To that end, we believe that two dimensions that have been somewhat neglected in Western theology can inspire us: the pneumatological dimension, in which the sacraments are seen as the continuous activity of God's Spirit, and the eschatological dimension, which regards the sacraments as prophetic signs from the perspective of their ultimate goal. We will pay explicit attention to both of these as amplifications of the christological and ecclesiological dimensions.

Any author knows that there are many other "authors" contributing to their text. I would like to recognize the splendid work of Dr. Marie Baird, Professor at Duquesne University, for her English translation of the Dutch text. Duquesne University made this translation possible by generously funding her work. I would also offer my sincere gratitude to Mrs. Britt Weynants from the secretariat of the Faculty of Theology, Catholic University of Leuven, for her typographical assistance and meticulous work in formatting the text. I would like to thank the editors, especially Nancy de Flon, Ph.D., at Paulist Press for their many insightful editorial suggestions and for publishing this text. Finally, I would like to thank Dr. George Worgul, Jr., for his efforts in revising this text for its English edition. He remains a much appreciated theological colleague and a dear friend.

FOREWORD

The Christian community has always proclaimed that Jesus who died is raised from the dead. The Christian community has likewise affirmed that the risen Lord has not abandoned the community of believers. No—the risen Lord is present. He is Emmanuel.

Throughout the ages, this presence of the risen Lord has been celebrated and experienced in the worship of the community. When we are gathered as two or three in the name of the Lord we experience as a free gift the saving love of Jesus in the concrete context of our lived experiences. In and through the celebration the presence of the Lord becomes even more real and powerful. How is this possible? How can the one who passed through the shadow of death be here now? Throughout the ages, the believing community has always answered that this has happened through the power of the Holy Spirit—the gift of the risen Lord poured out upon us.

Jesus' resurrection and the powerful Spirit are mysteries of faith. This does not mean that they are obtuse and impenetrable; nor does it imply that we cannot understand them. On the contrary, these mysteries are invitations to understand ever more deeply and ever anew. The mysteries of faith are inexhaustibly intelligible. The more we grasp their meaning and significance, the more we are grasped by their "infinity." It is the role of theology to try as best it can to meditate on, clarify, relate, explore, and participate in these mysteries of faith. Faith calls for the best of human efforts in reason, intuition, and imagination to participate ever more deeply in the mysteries of faith.

Participation is a crucial component in our relationship to the Christian mysteries. The real knowledge derived from experience can heighten, correct, and expand the notional knowledge that arises from history and academic study. Dr. Leijssen has clearly produced a text on the sacraments that is rooted in lived experience and profound theological study, reflection, and synthesis. He has given us a text that will assist theologians, clergy, theological students, pastoral ministers, catechists, and all who seek a better understanding of their faith to grasp the impact of postmodernity on liturgical sacramental life.

Sacraments are concrete lived experiences. They are always celebrations at a particular time, by a specific people, and in a concrete place. They are necessarily culture experiences. Anyone who has studied the history of any sacrament as lived in the churches recognizes how the needs, impulses, and presuppositions of a culture have shaped the celebration and understanding of that particular sacrament. When the Second Vatican Council's *Constitution on the Sacred Liturgy* called for an adaptation of the sacramental celebrations to the contexts and cultural conditions of the real people of every land, it was not issuing a "novel" teaching or creating a new enterprise in the church. On the contrary, adaptation and reform of worship and liturgy are the normative forces in the worshiping community as a real community—even though this may not be so apparent.

The need for adaptation in the liturgical sacramental life of the churches may not always be of the same intensity or magnitude. Different cultural shifts call for different responses. The signs of the times are not necessarily predictable. Often the adaptation is not a theological change but a cultural evolution that calls forth a new interpretation. There are other occasions, however, when the need for revision and reform is quite intense and comprehensive. I am convinced that we live in the latter age. In the West, we are in a transition from modernity to postmodernity, and the foundational principles as well as the institutional structures of culture are shaking.

Postmodernity should not be confused with postmodernism. The former is a description of a culture condition; the latter is a somewhat loosely connected set of ideas such as relativism, nihilism, or emotivism, which some have categorized as ideologies and inimical to Christian faith, although I am not certain that postmodernism is necessarily an ideology. The church's real concern must be with postmodernity, the cultural condition. The church has no choice but to try to understand this emerging cultural phenomenon as best it can, since it is the place where the faithful are living and where the gospel is to be preached. The risen Lord will also be present in the postmodern age, just as he has been in each age and place. In a special way, the liturgical sacramental life of the church will be a nodal point for the meeting of the gospel and postmodernity.

Interestingly, there are dimensions of postmodernity that resonate with dimensions of the Christian tradition: for example, apophatic theology, the openness and dynamism of the Christian story, the emphasis on God's love as pure gift, the desire for a community of ethics, the need for decontextualization and recontextualization, and so forth. How, then, do we understand and grasp the meaning, dynamic, and interrelationship of the Christian sacraments when they are experienced and viewed in this postmodern cultural context?

With the Silent Glimmer of God's Spirit: A Postmodern Look at the Sacraments is a fine introduction to the ongoing task of sacramental liturgical inculturation. After exploring the challenge facing liturgical sacramental theology in our present time, the text explores each of the sacraments by grouping them as sacraments of initiation, sacraments of healing, and sacraments of vocation. In a consistent manner the text offers a brief historical overview and then takes up the task of expressing the meaning of these holy gifts in the context of postmodernity.

There is kindness, wisdom, and courage in this book. Its author is very accurate in his historical explication, and he has a keen awareness of the forces that steered both the Christian community and its theologians to journey down the roads they have walked. The text is balanced and has a deep appreciation for the complexity of ecclesial sacramental life as lived in an increasingly complex world. But most of all, the text is courageous. It honestly faces the tradition and its history. It listens to the voices of contemporary believers who may be living in a "strange emerging world." It is hopeful and always points out the traces of the Holy Spirit, the presence of the risen Lord still moving in the world. The community of believers still celebrates together the sacred mysteries of faith. Professor Leijssen's text goes far in helping us better understand our lived experiences.

George S. Worgul, Jr.
Duquesne University, Pittsburgh

Chapter One
LIFE RITUALS: METAPHORIC CELEBRATIONS OF EXISTENCE

In my Father's house there are
many dwelling places.

(John 14:2)

Theological reflection on the current practice of the sacraments is best situated in an anthropological approach to ritual behavior. Christian sacraments share the aspect of ritual with all humankind's various religious rituals. The sacraments share this common point of departure with both sacred and secular rituals.

In this context, I am using the word *religious* in its broadest meaning, that is, "that which binds *(religare)* the person with the transcendent, the divine, or that which is higher or deeper, that which is other than oneself...." People of all times have experienced a relationship with the transcendent primarily by engaging in rituals. In and through rituals, people claim contact with these higher powers, to honor or control, to gain reconciliation, or to compel favors by bringing offerings. These ritual archetypes have to do with the experience of the natural world within which humans are physically situated and within which the transcendent is experienced.

The results of ethnographic empirical research on religious rituals, further examined by critical analysis in the philosophy of religion, cultural anthropology, semiotics, folklore, and linguistics, are of the utmost importance for sacramental theology. I share Edward Schillebeeckx's opinion concerning the amalgamation of the anthropological and the "theological" dimension directed to God in the sacraments, and I agree with him completely that the point of departure for a rediscovery of the Christian sacraments must be the "ritualization of religious moments in daily life."[1]

In summary, then, sacraments are comparable with other religious rituals, and they share a number of common characteristics and functions with them. I am thoroughly aware that "religion" cannot be equated with "belief." Ultimately, the specificity of the sacraments can be described only from the particular perspective of Christian faith. We will return to the topic of the particularity of the faith option, a typical characteristic of a postmodern approach. First, however, I would like to consider the relationship between religion and faith in the sacraments from the perspective of the celebration of the so-called rites of passage.

The Relationship between Religion and Faith

This question is an old one in theology. On the one hand, the most extreme position is represented by Karl Barth's rigid assertion that faith can be understood only as an answer to the divine revelation in Jesus; everything that is thought of as religion from below, from the human, is not Christian faith. On the other hand, we see the flowing, melting, gradual transition and purification of religious attitudes by authentic faith. This is a broad field with many questions that are posed by various disciplines, such as the philosophy of religion and theology.

Religious experience, however vague and unnuanced it may be, remains the starting point for research. Where does that peculiarly human experience come from? Why can the human person be named a *homo religiosus?* Isn't this a generally human and thus universal experience? All the world's religions can bear witness to the way these experiences are to be particularized. Such questions are connected with the concept of a Creator God, a possible revelation of the divine, providence, and a punishing or rewarding authority. They concern the immanent and/or transcendent character of the divine. Does the divine being remain a stranger to the visible world and divided from it, or is it interwoven with the world and invisibly present? Which religious expressions are trustworthy? Personally, I regard the theologian's task as one of further clarifying the religious

2

experiences of people, past and present, against the background of the testimonies of believers, prophets, and mystics. These testimonies can be recorded and handed down in texts, such as declarations of faith, around which a religion or a community of belief was formed and a tradition was built up. To which truth claims do these texts give witness?

In the beginning of my own study of the sacraments, I was strongly moved by a noteworthy text of Johann Wolfgang van Goethe (1749–1832) that was quoted by Otto Semmelroth in his book *Church and Sacrament*. The quotation is from Goethe's autobiography, *Aus meinem Leben: Dichtung und Wahrheit*. This text dates from the beginning of the nineteenth century and reflects the romanticism of the versatile poet who could sing so profoundly of human experience. I agree with Semmelroth's judgment that Goethe gives voice to a "catholic" vision in this text, although he did not belong to a particular church:

> In things ethical and religious, as well as in those physical and civic, man [*sic*] does not like to act extemporaneously; he needs a sequence on which habit can be based. That which he should love and do, he cannot think of alone and isolated; in order to want to repeat something, it must not have become strange to him....The sacraments are the high point of a religion, the visible symbol of an extraordinary divine favour and grace....Such a sacrament may not stand alone. No Christian can enjoy it with real joy for which it is given, unless the symbolic or sacramental sense has been nourished in him. He must be accustomed to see the interior religion of the heart and the external religion of the Church as one complete unity, as a great common sacrament that can be divided into many different parts, each of which gives its own holiness, indestructibility and immortality.[2]

Goethe continues by evoking all of life, from cradle to grave, and he indicates how, at important and decisive moments, a sacrament always brings to expression the most profound meaning of human occurrences. A certain *panentheism* can be discerned in

everything that is
is God

3

Goethe's vision, in which the divine is experienced simultaneously as immanent and transcendent. Semmelroth seizes upon this text in order to clarify further the order in the sevenfold sacraments of the church, which he characterizes as "fundamental sacrament."[3]

What particularly remained with me from this text was the unity between visible and invisible: "the visible symbol of an extraordinary divine favour and grace." The category of *symbol* forms a central understanding in every theology of the sacraments. The symbol possesses the capacity to "unite, bring together" (from the Greek *sym-ballein*) the visible and invisible orders. The sacrament as symbol does not refer to an absent reality; it calls forth the invisible, divine favor into visibility. In the experience of the sacraments we come in contact with the divine. The liturgical celebration links up with the human experience of divine proximity. A symbolization takes place in the liturgy of the sacraments that binds human occurrence with divine nearness. A transfer, a transposition takes place toward the divine. Schillebeeckx thinks of the sacraments "as metaphoric celebrations."[4] The deepest human experiences are transferred *(meta-ferein)* into the realm of the divine, and they become carriers of divine favor and grace.

Rites of Passage

An interesting test case of the relationship between religion and faith lies in the current association between the sacraments and *rites of passage*. Together with various researchers in the Catholic Documentation and Research Centre (Kadoc) in Leuven, we have established a series called "Life Rituals," in which rites of passage are defined as follows:

This series treats of those rituals that mark and interpret important moments in the life of a human being. It is about the description as well as the interpretation of these rituals. The functions that are exercised by these rituals are various: integration in a subgroup of the society, strengthening of the group mentality, tie with the tradition and expression of a certain religiosity. In this last function they give voice to a religious point of view with respect to the life experience, the point of contact of the transcendent, the holy, with ordinary life. The rituals that in sociology are called "rites of passage" mark the transition from a former phase to a new phase. Through these rituals, the individual receives a new status in the community. Characteristic of these rituals are the performative language and the use of symbols.[5]

Life rituals can be broken into four general phases: birth, growth, marriage, and end of life. In the Catholic community they are tied to baptism, confirmation, marriage, the anointing of the sick, and Christian burial. It is striking that, although many Catholics may seldom participate in the Eucharist on Sunday, they still request these "life rituals" at these four moments of transition. The situation of such believers, who are sometimes called "marginal churchgoers," raises serious questions for pastoral theology. In the eyes of pastors, these people often seem to ask for a "religious" interpretation, a ritualization of a liminal situation for which they find no better alternative than the ecclesial. In French, these celebrations are simply called *les fêtes des quatre saisons*, or "feasts of the four seasons." We want a feast to celebrate a birth. First communion and confirmation are feasts for the youth and their families. The engagement of a couple and their eventual marriage are celebrated in the marriage feast.[6] The celebrations of rites of passage are the pillars of a church community.

The French church faced the confrontation with secularization and lack of church affiliation earlier than elsewhere. This community developed various strategies for responding to this situation, ranging from low-threshold, mild pastorals of welcoming and invitation to a more demanding, high-threshold attitude that does not permit the sacraments to be "sold out" or offered indiscriminately. Sometimes correctly, pastors interpret the request in this way: the people are asking for a ritual, and we give them a sacrament that they actually do not know or understand. Advocates of an open "folk" Catholicism, such as Robert Pannet, hear the criticism that this approach offers only a temporary solution in the expectation that such people will completely leave the church. The church of the future must ask for a conscious faith decision in relation to the sacraments in order to stand firm in the middle of a pluralistic and secularized society and culture.[7]

In the church community in Belgium, we respond and experiment in nuanced and various ways in order to accompany the marginal churchgoers in a pastoral atmosphere of gradualness and initiation, as well as to protect the conscious choice in favor of the sacrament as a better alternative for the future of the church. I personally opt for a mild pastoral attitude of welcoming in which every opportunity is seized to allow the request for a sacrament to develop into a conscious choice, as far as possible. In that respect, I also understand one bishop's plea, against the grain, regarding a church of the future that is identified as nothing but "a particular group in society, a sign of God's universal grace and liberation." He advocates "radicalizing the ritual to its specifically Christian eloquence. At the same time, we can let them appreciate that more is at play than the occasional sacralization of a life moment, that it is ultimately about something that gives life itself a new direction."[8]

Perspectives

Placed in the context of postmodern culture, the vision of radicalizing religious ritual to its specifically Christian eloquence will become stronger. The *unsynchronous synchronicity* of cultural shifts has been noted by some.[9] The experience of the sacraments as rites of passage expresses an ambivalent attitude: On the one hand, we call upon a trusted ritual that originates in the tradition of a premodern culture; yet, even in modern culture there remains an unmistakable desire to ritualize important life moments. Viewed through an anthropological and cultural-philosophical lens, it is clear that, while rituals are necessary for a fulfilled life in a secularized culture, the modern individual moves in a "religious-symbolic vacuum."[10] The appeal to trusted rituals and symbols as remainders of a vanished civilization is an exponent of religiosity, but it must be framed within an initiation in and devotion to a real community. "The cry 'back to the rituals' arouses suspicion because it slips easily past an authentic intuition of the ritual: the religious tradition with its narratives of human origin and ultimate end, its evocations of the sacred and religious well-being. Ritual forms without religious tradition threaten to become empty and hollow very quickly."[11]

One sacramental theologian[12] reflects critically on our vision of *life* rituals:

> The fact is, the danger is not merely theoretical that Christian identity and the anthropological basis are so telescoped into one another that the one will lose out at the expense of the other. The identity of the sacrament will then dominate and manipulate the anthropological basis, or the opposite will happen: the anthropological basis will, as it were, swallow up the identity of the sacrament. After all, the connection between rites of passage and sacraments is not a necessary one.[13]

A French newspaper recently conducted an extensive survey in which it noted a halt in the decline in church attendance and in the destruction of the community of faith. These results offer a sign of hope: they "indicate a stabilization rather than a further deterioration. That more marginal believers are calling themselves Catholic once again teaches that faith, for many French, is more than what sociologists call 'remnant Christendom.'"[14] Perhaps what is needed is "a sort of 'wide angle pastoral' by which the large group of marginal believers, who seem to be seeking to approach the Church once again, isn't left out in the cold." It is wrong to take into account only the small "faithful" flock, just as it is to adopt a defeatist attitude and "resign oneself...to the indifference of the young."[15] A growth process is happening in the church community in which people are distancing themselves from a clerical position of authority or from the concept of the church as the dominant factor in culture and society. As a result, perhaps, the specifically Christian witness may emerge more clearly into the light of day.

Christian sacraments are surely not to be reduced to mere rites of passage. Yet there is clearly a certain analogy between the most important moments of life and the celebration of the sacraments as interpretations of the "new" (Christian) life story. In postmodern sacramental theology, the dimension of the ritualization of life or metaphoric celebration of existence must be affirmed and maintained as a permanent component.

Chapter Two

NEW VISIONS
IN SACRAMENTAL THEOLOGY

In traditional scholastic theology, the sacraments were defined as "efficacious means or causes that communicate the grace that they stand for." Aristotelian epistemology and metaphysics formed the philosophical context for theological reflection, with categories such as *materia–forma*, substance–accident, and *causa*. These means were made available to the faithful through the ministry of the sacraments. No one imagined the danger of this presumably innocent model. Sadly, it gave rise to a distorted understanding of the sacraments as automatic dispensers of grace—"grace machines."

As a corrective to this view, Edward Schillebeeckx, Karl Rahner, and Piet Fransen offered new models of vision of the sacraments and grace. These models have found generally widespread acceptance in the field of sacramental theology.

Edward Schillebeeckx:
Encountering God via Christ

Right from beginning of his teaching, in the 1950s, Schillebeeckx brought a renewal to the current Thomistic vision of the sacraments. By allowing Thomistic thought to confront modern culture, Schillebeeckx transformed it from a closed to a more open system. He manipulated the central categories of (French) existential phenomenology and personalism, through which the experience of the sacraments can no longer be conceived as an "administration of the means of grace" but rather as an "encounter with a person."[1] In the occurrence of an encounter there is always a double, reciprocal movement: that of offer and invitation on the one side and that of response and agreement on the other. Dialogue, contact, and communication are thereby possible.

Schillebeeckx grounded his model on the double movement of the doctrine of redemption in Thomism: that of the descent (*exitus*) of God in the sanctification (offer) and the return (*reditus*) of the individual in worship. Jesus is the primordial exemplar of this dynamic. He offers salvation as God and gives the perfect response in obedience as a human being. This mystery finds its continuation in the ecclesiastical sacraments, the earthly continuation of the heavenly mystery of Christ. Sacraments are ecclesial acts that render visible the presence of the glorified humanity of Christ (*humanitas Christi*). The sacraments offer salvation in the name of God and witness the human response in faith through thanksgiving, gratitude, and praise.

Schillebeeckx's vision heralded a groundbreaking renewal. The sacraments were no longer understood as mere objects that dispensed grace to passive recipients when performed by legitimate ecclesiastical ministers. This new vision undeniably brought into high relief the active role of the faithful. Their attitude of response in faith is an integral part of the sacramental pattern.

The main point of Schillebeeckx's approach lies in Christology. Erik Borgman, who has studied Schillebeeckx's theology, characterizes this vision as follows: "The human individual was personified by the divine Word; the 'function of person' of this individual was 'exercised by the divine person himself.'" In other words, Schillebeeckx was convinced that Jesus Christ was human in a divine manner. But of even greater importance was the contrary thought that finally formed the basis for his vision of God as *Deus humanissimus*. According to Schillebeeckx, what took place in Christ most profoundly was a "humanizing of God": "God is human and allows himself to be known as God in the form of a concrete human life."[2] In this context Schillebeeckx developed the vision of Jesus as a special sacrament that he calls the mystery of Christ, "the original sacrament, from which the Christian sacraments become intelligible."[3] Here, the term *original sacrament* should be interpreted in line with the early Christian meaning of *mysterion*: "revelation of the divine mystery." As human, Jesus simultaneously revealed God in his life, death, and resurrection and responded to this revelation in perfect worship, his voluntary self-sacrifice. He is, in one person, the definitive revelation of God and the paradigm of human response.

Karl Rahner: Highest Degree of Proclamation of the Word

Karl Rahner's theological efforts to reformulate scholastic theology appeared contemporaneously with Schillebeeckx's vision of the mystery of Christ as the original sacrament and Otto Semmelroth's proposal of the church as the fundamental sacrament. Rahner would reexamine the classical data of theology in terms of existential structures and foundations of human existence. In a sense, then, Rahner saw an intrinsic relationship between the mystery of God and the mystery of the human, between theodicy and theological anthropology. He arrived at "a theological anthropology on existential foundations."[4]

Two phases can be discerned in Rahner's vision of sacraments. In his early works he placed sacramental theology at the intersection and convergence of various theological disciplines.[5] He recognized that it was precisely in the experience of the sacraments that so many aspects come up for discussion. For example, sacramental theology is situated at the heart of ecclesiology as a discipline that connects with Christology and soteriology as the teaching of the historically and socially ongoing presence of the Christ event. The sacraments are the highest expression of being of the church. During this first phase of his thinking, Rahner understood the church as the original sacrament. The ecclesial dimension is decisive. Upon deeper reflection on the connection between Christ and the church, we see a refinement in the terminology and hence a better description of the connection. In fact, only Christ himself can be considered to be the origin (*origo, Ur*) of the sacraments. The church furthers the saving work of Christ in the sacraments. Rahner later gave the church the specific name of *Grundsakrament*, foundational sacrament.

From 1970 on, a new accent comes to the forefront for Rahner. Starting from an ecumenical approach, he defines the sacrament as the highest degree of proclamation of the word that is performed in the name and the commission of the church. Using the proclamation of the word as his point of departure, Rahner bridges the centuries-old opposition between "word" and "sacrament" as found in the tension between the Catholic and Protestant communions. In this tension, the reception of the sacraments was most important to Roman Catholics, whereas for Protestants it was the proclamation of the word that is received in faith.

Rahner placed himself in the Protestants' camp by also regarding the proclamation of the word to be the most important. The church is not only the bearer of God's proclaimed word; it is simultaneously and inseparably the faithful recipient of this word. God's self-revelation is irreversibly and definitively entrusted to the church in history after Christ, not for itself as church, but rather as a sign of salvation for the world. In this way, we can call the church a complete sacrament, an active sign and instrument of salvation for the world, a historical appearance of God's grace in a world that is heading toward the final culmination of God's kingdom, which is irreversibly present.

The Christian sacraments are thus the highest forms of realization, the highest level of grace in the word, which are promised to the faithful in decisive moments of life. In this context, "word" may be interpreted as the incarnate Word of God, Jesus Christ. The redemptive paschal mystery of Christ is promised in each sacrament and really experienced by the community of faith together. Rahner has freed the sacraments from the narrow bonds of the scholastic concept of "sign and cause of grace." He abandoned the pretense that the profane world had never previously experienced the grace communicated to it in sacraments.

Rahner offers a very broad interpretation of grace as God's self-communication of love to the entire world. In this connection Rahner speaks of a Copernican revolution. The world is already profoundly penetrated by grace in its very origins *(im Daseinsgrund)*. The cosmos is a reality inspired by God from its very creation. This grace comes explicitly to the surface in revelation in history with Jesus Christ as its culminating point, and it becomes real in the response of the faithful. The grace that is already present is manifested in sacramental celebrations and tied to the mystery of Christ. They are thus the highest form of expression of Christ's proclamation for the salvation of the world. In that sense they are also prophetic signs: a seizing in advance of the coming of God's kingdom.

The actualization of grace in the sacraments may not be regarded as a mere "infusion" of a grace conceived as real. Grace is a relational, dynamic reality; it is a real participation in the love bond of the Three In One. As signs of faith, the sacraments are not only remembrances of Christ *(signa rememorativa)* and actual, personal, intersubjective encounters with Christ *(signa demonstrativa)*. They are also and especially signs of completed salvation *(signa prognostica)*. Here Rahner follows Thomas Aquinas's vision, but he improves on it by overcoming the division between sign and origin in one term: *Realsymbol*. The reality experienced in the sacrament is simultaneously the symbol or sign of the most profound, invisible union with God. Rahner notices that Thomas's eschatological meaning was clear, but that modern sacramental theology must rediscover and develop this dimension anew. He emphasized the "now," the "already" aspect of the ultimate salvation in the celebration of the sacraments. Present experiences can be completely understood only from the perspective of the eschatological future. This should be interpreted precisely as dogmatic theologian Lieven Boeve has correctly noted:

> The end time is no dramatic era out there in the future, but is rather taking place right here and now. Jesus has already come—in the fundamental decision that individuals make with regard to their existential orientation: believe, and thus elude personal fallen-ness and sinful highhandedness, or not. For Karl Rahner, "apocalyptic" is a test word to indicate badly understood eschatology. The term points to the reportage-like prophecy of things that will happen at the end of history. Real eschatology does not prophesy but rather enables one to foresee. In this way the individual experiences his or her present as his or her "definitive future hidden in the present and already offering him salvation now if it is accepted as the deed of God the only ruler, the time and manner of which remain incalculable."[6]

In this connection Rahner speaks of a "cosmic" history of grace. The grace that has been offered since creation itself remains real as an inner dynamic pointing toward the ultimate destination. Rahner expresses this with the Aristotelian term *entelechy* (*en-telos*, directed toward the final goal). Grace is visibly present as long as the individual does not oppose God in a genuinely deliberate "no," thus cutting him- or herself off from the God who offers salvation. According to Rahner, this grace becomes visible, even anonymously, in the concrete history of people who live and die without a mortal kind of guilt. He describes the world as a place in which the human person, bestowed with spiritual capacities, freely accepts or declines the pardon proffered in God's name. For Rahner, the refusal does not yet signify a denial of the offer. The world is, to its very roots, borne up by God's self-communication and propelled toward its ultimate destination. This is not a so-called profane world that the sacraments must infiltrate as pointed interventions from outside, made in God's name; rather, this is the world that God has pardoned. Grace is not communicated through the sacraments as extraordinary phenomena that intervene in a special manner outside of everyday life. Grace is the final depth and radicality of everything that the individual experiences concretely.

Clearly, Rahner is following the spirituality of Ignatius of Loyola, that is, to see and find God in everyday situations. Rahner is also familiar with the conceptual universe of his fellow Jesuit Pierre Teilhard de Chardin regarding the liturgy of the world. An inner dynamic is active in normal, "profane" life that emanates from God and is propelled back to God. This inner dynamic is most highly and clearly visible in Jesus of Nazareth, the definitive and unsurpassable Word of God, addressed to the person who either explicitly or implicitly responds in faith. In this manner the Christian sacraments become the form of appearance, the visible holiness of humans and the world. They are grace in explicitly visible form. Real life is celebrated in the liturgical act. Christ's cross is not raised anew, but his hidden, lasting presence in the world is proclaimed anew. In this way, the celebration of the sacraments places the believer within the dynamic of the pardoned world, in the depth of God's self-communication, in the history of salvation under way to its ultimate outcome. The sacraments are not empty ceremonies or formal, superfluous rites. They are the way in which grace itself appears. If one desires to determine the activity of the sacraments, one need search no further than the sign itself. In this context Rahner speaks of the *Realsymbol's* causality of the sign. Once again, he rejects the division that Thomas established between sign and cause. The sign is active in itself because it is the expression of the deeper reality. This sign is experienced as an action, constituted by free human beings at the decisive moments of their lives.

Rahner says himself that the central point of his entire theology can be nothing else than the proclamation of God as mystery and Jesus Christ, crucified and resurrected, as the one in whom the irreversible coming of this God has occurred historically in its highest self-communication. He excluded from his final writings any references to the world as alien territory. Contemporary theology is about discovering God's salvation-in-the-world, God's already present, liberating activity wherever loving, just, and honest living takes place and where the church, as a sacrament for the world, is assigned the role of bringing the traces of God's presence more strongly to the surface and pointing explicitly in reference to, and anchoring in, the mystery of Christ's death and resurrection. The sacraments stand in the church as the explicit, concrete form of appearance of God's activity in Christ, here and now, as signs to the world. They are expressions of the power of the Spirit that is active in the dynamism toward the ultimate end.

Rahner himself did not work out the pneumatological dimension of the sacraments thematically, although the means of doing so were available. That was accomplished by theologians who were trained by him, such as Walter Kasper, Raphael Schulte, Christian Schütz, Peter Hünermann, Arno Schilson, and Alexander Ganoczy.[7]

Sacraments Are Communal Celebrations

Postconciliar theology has incorporated research from the human sciences, a tendency characterized by Antoon Vergote as "the anthropological turn."[8] The human person, with his or her possibilities and manifestations, holds a central place. This shift has

15

led to the highlighting of liturgical ritual as a human undertaking. The point of departure is no longer God, who remains in the center and approaches humanity. The sacramental liturgy is convened from the perspective of the individual who steps before God in the community of faith. In this scheme, expression becomes the centrally important conceptual category.[9]

Various forms of expression are available: the language of prayer and song, the language of the body, the totality of the human person in the community that expresses and symbolizes the relationship with God. By this means, faith is brought to experience in liturgical acts that are posited gratuitously to oneself with no other ulterior motive than to express one's faith. Surrounded and borne by the entire community, each believer gives shape and space to his or her personal relation to God in the liturgy. This expression of faith is brought to experience and strengthened by the communal witnessing of the entire community.

Antoon Vergote leads the way by characterizing the liturgy as a cult celebration:

> One celebrates a festal occasion: something important that takes place, which happens to one as a salvific reality. Two elements thus belong to the celebration: what takes place is recognized by an individual as a specifically human occurrence, and this occurrence possesses the characteristic of the gratuitous gift that lifts the individual above daily worry and labor and gives him or her a higher sense of human worth or a greater sense of life fulfillment. In this way, one celebrates a person whose exceptional activity has given new worth to the community; or one celebrates on a day of remembrance a meaningful occurrence from the history of a people. That which is celebrated is always an occurrence that brings new meaning. Thus, the cult is also a celebration, because one remembers God's miracles and in so doing interiorizes them again as still present and active.[10]

In this sense, we can speak of the sacraments as celebrations, festal observances in thankfulness, praise, and joy.

In the vision of Piet Fransen, the model of communal celebration also deserves particular attention in his search for the most suitable model for our time.[11] In addition to other motives for his preference for this model in sacramental theology, he mentions the movement characterized by Robert Pannet as a Catholicism of the people or "folk Catholicism."[12] A pastoral approach to the so-called seasonal Christians, marginal churchgoers, has revealed how much importance should be given to the festal character of the sacraments for believers who want to remain connected to the church in a less intellectually or immediately engaged manner. The liturgical celebration is to be a festal moment in an otherwise flat, dull existence. This festal character is promoted by means of true beauty, music, images, architecture, symbolic expressions that touch the entire person.

Fransen also develops a sacramental model of celebration from his vision of grace as the loving presence of God in the most profound part of our selves. We celebrate what we most intimately are. We celebrate, in joy, God's proximity in the community of faith. We celebrate the benefits, the divine mysteries, that are revealed in Jesus and his people, in the experience of the kingdom of God that is in our midst. In this approach, which Fransen called the mystical way, we give space to deep feelings of joy, freedom, fulfillment, praise, and thankful gratitude. The faithful experience themselves as overflowing with God's love. They recognize themselves as children of one Father, brought together in the community of the church. When we approach the community celebrating Eucharist as a community of active persons, then the aspects of festivity, joy, thankfulness, and the building of community must also be borne by everyone.

The celebrational model of sacramental theology has been introduced to the English-speaking world in the work of George Worgul.[13] As metaphors of existence, the sacraments raise daily life to a spiritual level. They are symbolic actions, transpositions of the life of faith into the liturgical realm. In the work of sacramental theologian Louis-Marie Chauvet, the symbolic comes completely into the foreground. A symbolic order comes into being through the sacraments, a coherent network *(réseau)* of signs that supports and maintains all of Christian life. Chauvet distances himself from ontotheology, which works with abstract concepts, and prefers to replace such concepts with a symbolic order that is rooted in concrete physicality, offering space for the Word event in the explicitly Christian proclamation of the Jesus story.[14] His approach may be regarded as a reformulation of the Christian manner of living in a postmodern culture.

A Perspective from Liberation Theology

Latin American liberation theologians draw our attention to the necessary connection between sacramental celebrations and the social stakes, justice and hope in situations of suffering. Francisco Taborda connects praxis and festivity.[15] Sacraments are *kairos*-moments in life, festivals that mark off an otherwise chaotic time and impart deeper meaning to both happy and tragic occurrences. Taborda is attentive to the simplest of believers, the "poor," who often regard popular devotion as the only outlet to express their faith and trust, thus finding support and hope in order to survive.

In his first phase as a liberation theologian, Leonardo Boff put forth a remarkable vision of the sacramentality of all of existence, referring to a deeper meaning for those who want to be open to it and who want to enter the story.[16] His sacramental theology, formulated in the framework of a narrative theology, remains extremely valuable, even if in his further development he personally lost trust in the church as an institution of power. In later chapters, some of his thoughts will be developed in conjunction with the remaining new accents in contemporary sacramental theology.

Chapter Three

THE SEVEN SACRAMENTS

There are many religious rituals, but there are only seven sacraments. Certain rituals have gradually been acknowledged as sacraments in the life of the ecclesial community. Life happened first and theory followed afterwards. In the earliest phase, just after the crucifixion and resurrection of Jesus, the memory of Jesus was celebrated in the Eucharist and new members were admitted to the Christian community through baptism. Baptism and Eucharist are thus the first and most important sacraments.

In the course of history other rituals were acknowledged as belonging to the central celebrations of the ecclesial community whereby the paschal mystery of Christ was commemorated. Among the various liturgical celebrations, prayers, and blessings, seven "sacred signs" were ultimately classified with the technical name of "sacrament." This process of acknowledgment culminated in the theology of Peter Lombard (1095–1160) and, further, in the official doctrine of the church as established in the councils of Florence (1439) and Trent (1547). Scholastic theology had a clear definition of the sacrament as "a visible sign of an invisible grace." Proceeding from this definition, a systematic doctrine of the seven central rites was developed: baptism, confirmation, Eucharist, reconciliation, anointing of the sick, marriage, and holy orders. This historical development must not blind us to the fact that each of these sacraments had its own preliminary history and separate meaning.

Sacraments and Pivotal Life Moments

Further reflection on the seven sacraments leads to the insight that, in fact, the important moments of life are connected to a sacrament. Leonardo Boff clarifies the historical choice of the seven sacraments by attributing them to a more profound intuitive feeling that exists at a structurally unconscious level. He remarks:

> If we look closely, we shall see that on the ritual level the seven sacraments express the pivotal points of human life. There are key moments in life, especially in its biological dimensions. There are nodal points in life where the crucial lines of the transcendent meaning of the human being meet and cross. At these points human beings sense that their lives are not self-sustaining. They possess life, but they have received it....These nodal points in life take on an eminently sacramental character, and so we surround them with symbols and rites....These nodal points are the sacraments of life *par excellence* because in them is transparently condensed the life of the sacraments: the presence of the Transcendent, of God.[1]

In this way, we can say that the seven sacraments unfold and sublimate the principal moments of life.

This vision has been incorporated into the official doctrine as formulated, for example, in the *Apostolic Constitution on the Sacrament of Confirmation* of Paul VI: "The partnership in the divine nature, with which the human person is enriched through the grace of Christ, exhibits a certain conformity to the origin, growth and nurturance of the natural life. Reborn through baptism, the faithful are strengthened by the sacrament of confirmation and nourished by the Eucharist. Through these sacraments of Christian initiation, they participate more and more in the treasures of the divine life and progress on the path of perfect love."[2]

The *Catechism of the Catholic Church* also expresses this insight: "The seven sacraments touch all the stages and all the important moments of Christian life: they give birth and increase, healing and mission to the Christian's life of faith. There is thus a certain resemblance between the stages of natural life and the stages of the spiritual life."[3]

A network, as it were, of symbolic celebrations is spread over all of life by the seven sacraments. The deeper meaning of the spiritual dimension of life's important occurrences is clarified by these celebrations. That is what is meant when Louis-Marie Chauvet speaks of a symbolic network in which the individual tracks down the proper plan of life and its point of connection with the transcendent.[4]

Life Moments

Infant baptism is the first important moment in the symbolic order, the beginning and foundation of the sacramental structure of life. Baptism means rebirth in the paschal mystery of Christ, being a child of God and becoming incorporated into the visible ecclesial community. Confirmation affirms growth in the Christian life with a renewed gift of the Holy Spirit and a closer connection to the church community. Both sacraments form the foundation of the common priesthood of the faithful, in which the faithful share in Christ's priesthood in order to offer God true worship and to bear witness to the evangelical message.

In the Eucharist, the central sacrament of the seven, the Christian encounters the glorified Christ in the remembrance of his Word and his paschal mystery, and he or she is fed with the bread of eternal life. In a real sense all of the sacraments flow from and lead to the Eucharist, the central mystery of our faith and the core meaning of the person and mystery of Jesus, the Christ.

The sacraments of reconciliation and anointing of the sick accompany the experiences of wounded existence, as much in the moral sense of sinfulness as in the physical meaning. They bring to bear a vision of the end of life, of ultimate destiny, on these experiences of limitedness and sinfulness. Through the forgiveness of sins, the Christian is liberated from guilt by the merits of Christ's redemptive paschal mystery. In the anointing of the sick, the believer receives the consolation and strength to bind his or her suffering to that of the crucified Lord and the promise of the expectation of eternal life in commitment to the risen Lord.

There are also two sacraments that sanctify one's state in life. Marriage and holy orders celebrate a faithful commitment of adults in view of the building up of the church and the experience of God's fidelity. In the sacrament of holy orders, the believer shares in Christ's priesthood, in the specific sense of Christ, the head of the church, with the tasks of guidance, proclamation, and leadership in worship. Marriage, as the sacrament that sanctifies a relationship, unites the couple as having been given to each other with the most profound divine bond: their yes to each other is anchored in the promise of God's covenant with humanity. In the reflection on the deeper meaning of this commitment as we find it in the letter to the Ephesians (5:21–33), the marriage relationship is compared to Christ's surrender to his ecclesial community: the union of man and wife reflects the selfless love of Christ, who remained true to his calling even on the cross. The newly married are thus called to love each other according to the example of Jesus and in the power of the Holy Spirit, with the same selfless love and fidelity that Jesus himself manifested. They sanctify each other in their love because they accomplish their human love in the bosom and power of divine love. This commitment marks them for life as eternally bound to each other in God's love and fidelity.[5]

Clearly, the life of the human person from birth to death contains ritual celebrations at decisive, liminal moments. These celebrations clarify the meaning of life in the context of Christian belief. The sacraments are markers in the history of a person of faith. Through the sacraments, the Christian's journey through life becomes sealed with the paschal mystery of Christ.

Chapter Four
SACRAMENTAL PRESENCE IN A POSTMODERN CONTEXT

For with you is the fountain of life;
and in your light we see light.
(Psalm 36:9)

Contemporary philosophers and theologians use the term *postmodern* to characterize the contemporary cultural climate. This term points to the disintegration of the overall connectedness and overarching sense of coherent meaning, "the end of the grand metanarratives" (Lyotard).[1] The preference seems to be for the particular, the emotional, the aesthetic, and the playful. "It is as if the world in all its aspects threatens to fall to pieces."[2]

It is undeniable that present-day culture exhibits a pluralism and a blurring of values.[3] This is what happens when we no longer realize that we belong to a "mystical body," "a special kind of union that humans are unable to forge themselves."[4] This mystical body is a tissue of relations, bonds of loyalty, a connectedness in which individuals and groups receive identity and direction: "The postmodern individual thinks that he or she can rise above this tissue in a consciously superior manipulation of the symbols and signs that were left over for one or another reason."[5]

The Postmodern Condition

The term *postmodern* has a number of possible connotations.[6] In the research project on postmodern sacramental theology that my colleagues and I undertook at the Catholic University of Leuven (KUL) in 1996, we were able to proceed from a *status quaestionis* that an unmistakable caesura is noticeable in current philosophical and theological thought. The status of metaphysics has been called into question in its ability to articulate the "most profound levels of reality."[7] Not only premodernity, with the naive open-mindedness of a mythical and pre-Copernican worldview, but also the rational insights of the Enlightenment and the "new theology" that attempted to integrate this modern rationality deserve to be subjected to a hermeneutical critique.

As far as the sacraments are concerned, it is striking that the premodern conceptual categories from the scholastic, Thomistic synthesis are still current, with Aristotelian metaphysics forming the supporting conceptual structure. This structure was called into question by the Reformation, with a (temporary) answer from the Council of Trent. In ecumenical dialogue this framework often remains in effect.

Before being able to concentrate on the operation of the individual sacraments, we had to work out a concept that would enable us to understand sacramentality in a broad sense, including the sacramentality of the world. In postmodern culture, after the end of the grand metanarratives and the collapse of ideologies, we can no longer speak of God by simply affirming God's "presence" in creation. Modern, instrumental rationality already had difficulties with that. In today's postmodern thought world, when we search for possible ways of speaking about God's presence, we see that it will always be in terms of absent/present, veiled/unveiled, transcendent/immanent, invisible/visible. Naturally, the mediation among these terms occurs along the lines of symbolicity, reference, call, meaning, and sacramentality. God cannot be experienced directly, but God probably can be experienced as "present absence." How this can be *reflexively* formulated and accepted in theological discourse forms the starting point for a postmodern sacramental theology. Georges De Schrijver took up this challenge in his address on November 4, 1999, at the opening of the international congress Leuven Encounters in Systematic Theology (LEST II).[8]

In this address, De Schrijver emphatically points out the distance between the visible world and the divine. With the (possible) acknowledgment of the sacramentality of existence, he stresses that we must not direct our attention to holy sites or moments at first. Already in modernity we witness the "disenchantment of the world"[9] by means of a radical empiricism and secularization that still preserve rituals as remainders of holy symbols in a deceptive manner. He calls upon the concept of the dialectic from Hegel's philosophy *(Aufhebung)*, which points to the abolition of the prior situation as well as to its hidden, persistent survival. If God can still be thought of as being present, then it is only under the covered, hidden form of an original language where only "traces" can be discovered in the distance that always exists between reality on the one hand and written language on the other (as Jacques Derrida noted with reference to negative theology). Together with Leonardo Boff, De Schrijver sees the world again as the horizon of experiences within which the divine can be pointed out.

Nowadays there is a change. Given the existential uncertainties and ambivalences of postmodernity, a simple transparency is no longer recognizable. The sacred (divine) can only be discovered in the experience of incompleteness and the contingency of the human race. The space of emptiness and distance is the place to find God again.

Here we must avoid a symmetrical relation between the knower and the known. In symmetry, God would become an object of our knowledge and our desire and thus would become an idol "in our image." Together with Jean-Luc Marion, De Schrijver rejects this reduction. Instead they both choose the inversion of the relation so that the human person acknowledges God's gift in radical openness and receptivity.[10] God has become an "icon" in the incarnate Word, through whom the divine light radiates to the human heart and spirit.[11]

Critique of Classical Sacramental Theology

In his critical observations with regard to the classical sacraments and sacramentality, De Schrijver refers this asymmetrical relation with regard to God to the asymmetry that exists mutually between people. He is able to connect indignation—Dorothee

Sölle's silent scream at the injustice in society—with John of the Cross's dark night of the soul, the emptiness where God is experienced.[12] The sacramentality of existence is truncated, clipped, and lopped off, and somewhere along this painful degeneration the individual is able to discern the presence of the true God. Therefore, only in the unconditional solidarity for a nonviolent struggle against injustice in this world by a horizontal praxis of liberation, and by breaking open the totalizing thought in a vertical line toward an (ontologically) good origin, can the reflection about God, as the echo of praxis and experience, result in the acknowledgment of the gratuitous nature of existence.

Personally, I use Louis Dupré's term *late modernity* to characterize the present reflection, which is associated with postmodernity.[13] The possibilities of human rationality have not weakened in this period, but we have become aware of the excesses of hyperrationality. In this sense, the term *late modernity* gives voice to the fact that a critical reflection on modernity has become necessary. According to Dupré, after the deconstruction by modernity we are left with the splinters of a broken mirror.[14] The reflective relationship, the symmetry, has indeed been disposed of. However, a new insight and a new point of view can develop from the fragmentary mirroring of the splinters (traces). Indeed, an inversion of our point of view can convert us to iconicity. We are no longer stuck in the reduction of the image of God as an idol of our desires, but we become open to the gaze of God upon creation and the human being. The gap between our knowing subjectivity and the object of our knowledge remains and may not be filled with representations. That is the space of emptiness, difference, *kenōsis*.

World as Gift

If, in the inversion of our point of view, we see the world as God's gift, creation, in which God gives himself to us and opens himself in self-emptying, then it is possible to conceive of sacramentality *reflexively-rationally* as a "present absence" of the divine, as a continuous glimpse (*glimmer*, not *glitter*),[15] a soft, silent splendor, a mild illumination of the withdrawing Mystery. That "dark" light reaches the believer (mystic) in the night of the senses and in structural-ethical conduct as the response, in faith, to the unconditional goodness of God, granted to us in creation. The experience of the world remains the horizon (Boff) where God approaches us. This experience asks for interpretation, not from need or want or from our illusions or projections. Rather, as Jean-Luc Marion has pointed out, God comes as an approaching gift *(don)*, to which we respond in prayer, resistance, and surrender *(abandon)*. The conscious experience that this world is given to us places the believer in a position of the one to whom is given *(l'adonné)*,[16] in which the true relationship with God can be experienced authentically.

The world can be sacramentally experienced as emanation, communication of God's goodness, God's language. Both Pierre Teilhard de Chardin and Karl Rahner described creation as *le milieu divin* with the radiation of God's love, in the emptying or *kenōsis* of God's love, evolving toward fulfillment at the end of time *(entelecheia)*.

At the origins *(im Daseinsgrund)*, "nothingness" cannot be foundational. Thus, a divine initiative is not unthinkable. De Schrijver correctly looks for a metaphysical explanation, also within (or as a critique of) postmodernity. This appeal to a metaphysical origin seems justifiable to him. Even though postmodernity rejects various forms of metaphysical-ontological thought, such as causality, the *analogia entis*, and the spiritual as the representation of a physical model, it does not follow it that denies a metaphysical origin of the world. In this sense, postmodernity should be interpreted not as antimetaphysical, but rather as postmetaphysical.

A Perspective from Schmemann and Chauvet

In reflecting on the sacramentality of the world, I personally find the Orthodox theology of Alexander Schmemann's standard work *The World as Sacrament* to be of particular worth.[17] While this work acknowledges an ontological basis for the symbolic structure of creation,[18] his emphasis lies, rather, in the eschatological directionality toward the completion of the new creation through liturgy, looking ahead toward the final cosmic fulfillment.

In this Eastern vision, following the Platonic thought of Dionysius the Areopagite, the symbol (sacrament) is experienced differently from the way it is experienced in Western models. The relation between symbol (manner of appearance) and reality is such that both may be conceptualized together as one whole, in tension (antinomy) to be sure, but not such that the more profound reality is regarded as being "absent," as is seen in the Western vision of representation through symbols. In this respect, Schmemann can describe the created world unproblematically as the sacrament of God's presence, in the context of his vision of creation, redemption, and *eschaton*, the fulfilled kingdom of God.

Reliance on symbolic structure is central to Louis-Marie Chauvet's sacramental theology. In his renewed (postmodern) thought about sacraments, he fills in ontological and conceptual discourse with terms from the symbolic order. He sees as equally worthwhile the possibility of arguing the truth claims that metaphysical discourse constructs by calling upon symbolic thought. In so doing, we avoid the contradictions inherent in ontological thinking with regard to God, and we can track down the true God, as revealed in the history of salvation and particularly in Jesus.

In order to incorporate this *reflexively* into Western thinking, we must take the scholastic tradition into account. This will not happen without "interruption" and "differential thinking": presence in difference.[19] In the Western vision, moreover, the eschatological perspective has never been conclusive. Sacramental theology was primarily considered from the perspective of the incarnation (*humanitas Christi*), continued in the sacraments of the church.

The narrative that Chauvet develops paradigmatically in order to support the turn toward a sacramental theology concerned with symbol is the Emmaus story of the breaking of the bread. Here the disciples recognize Jesus after his disappearance (the umpteenth *kenōsis*) in that emptiness and open space.[20] This active gesture of "breaking" is to be interpreted in the same manner as in Jean-Luc Marion's thought about the "given" (*donation*). It establishes a relation and constitutes the identity of the participants in the occasion as being involved in the most profound reality.

Chapter Five

SACRAMENT: THE LANGUAGE
OF THE SELF-GIVING GOD

We have established that one of the most important characteristics of a postmodern approach is the inversion of our point of view. A decentering of the "I" (Ego) takes place. God, who is known as the wholly Other, different from ourselves, looks at us human beings. It is no longer the person who looks at God as if looking at an image. Here is the difference between the icon and the idol. As icon, it is God who comes to us in the image as totally gratuitous gift to and for us. We experience ourselves as being loved by God, endowed with the gift of God's love, which is expressed most intensely in the person of Jesus. In an idol, we fill in the image with our own expectations and desires. The "god" we create is a mere idol, a false god or ourselves as gods.

The fundamental distinction between icon and idol, together with the idea of the free, gratuitous gift in the name of God, is central to the visions of Jean-Luc Marion and Louis-Marie Chauvet. David Power adopted it in his text on sacramental theology, *Sacrament, Language of God's Giving*, in which he provides a synthesis of what postmodern sacramental theology currently has to offer.

Power uses the present participle of the active verb "self-giving": God's oblatory, gratuitous self-giving in Christ and the Spirit actually occurs to us here and now. This looks like a symbolic occurrence (event) in language that, together with the distance and difference between written text and spoken word, generates the meaningful signification of the self-giving God in the paschal mystery of God's Word. This current presence of God includes the dimensions of remembering the events of salvation from the past and anticipating the definitive eschatological fulfillment.

29

Epistemologically, this knowledge comes to us via our images of God, idols. But the phenomenology that Marion is developing shows, philosophically as well, that ultimately the acknowledgment of God's gift takes precedence and happens first. The believer experiences and assents that this attitude of faith is God's self-giving. The believer finds him- or herself in the position of the one to whom is given. God looks at us *first* in the icon.

Power adopts this phenomenology of self-giving in his sacramental theology. In a hermeneutic of trust, not suspicion, he develops his theology as one of liturgical celebration that happens to us here and now, an "economy of gift."[1] Here, one starts from neither a metaphysical nor a subjective foundation. The point of departure lies fully in the conscious acknowledgment that the gift has preceded us in purely gratuitous self-communication. The sacraments are the language of this gift.

Language

In the first place, "language" is to be understood structurally as "medium," a mediation of mutual relations, the communicative act that establishes a personal relation between the parties involved in the process of communication. As the form of appearance of the encounter between God and the believer, language includes various components in ritual, more than just the spoken word. There is an entire gamut of extraverbal communication in liturgical celebrations: the sacred place with all its visual elements, the moments of silence, the music, the physical expressions in bearing and movement, the prayerful atmosphere....

The spoken word is endowed with an eminent role because, precisely in line with Karl Rahner's vision of the sacraments as the highest degree of the proclamation of the Word, the proclamation of our faith in the risen Christ occurs here. The verbal aspect is broader than what was formerly indicated by the *forma* of the sacrament, the key words that constitute the sacrament together with the *materia*. The liturgical celebration is important from beginning to end as a means of establishing the range of and participation in the sacramental occurrence.

The rules of good communication deserve to be respected here. The insights from linguistics and theories of communication are relevant: a clear and intelligible formulation of the content of the message by the sender, expressed in a code that can be decoded by the recipient based on his or her own background; the interaction between sender and recipients; the rhythm of offer and approval; the feedback from the recipient to the sender and vice versa. In liturgical communication it is exceptionally important to take into account that we are concerned with a special form of communication, namely, that the objective is rooted in the assumption that its goal is communication with the invisible God. Theories of communication speak of a "non-empirical referent." This places particular demands on liturgical language. I am referring here to "analogical" communication, in which we aim for attitudes that are paired with emotions, along with "digital" communication, which transmits information. The involvement of all the participants in the sacramental celebration is promoted by well-constructed forms of communication.

The liturgy of the sacraments is a language-*action*, an occurrence that realizes something. By means of language and the mutual relations that are created in this way, the original meaning of the sacrament is generated anew. What the church aims at with this sacrament, in line with Jesus' significance as origin and source of the sacraments, is actualized anew in favor of those participating in the liturgical event. Liturgical language is *performative:* it makes real what is being spoken. Liturgical language is *metaphorical:* it binds the visible reality to the deeper, spiritual reality that is indeed invisible to our eyes. Liturgy speaks about and to the Invisible.

The Invisible is revealed or disclosed to the inner eye of the heart. In this sense, liturgical language is related to *poetic* language: it calls forth, speaks to the imagination, touches the inner life. Comprehension, understanding, and illumination arise on the spiritual level. The South African poet and theologian Cas Vos speaks of metaphor as "sparks of imagination" in a field of tension between concrete space on the one hand and what is inaccessible to sight on the other.

When we look with the eye of the *imagination*, a *real* experience of presence, encouragement, and consolation is established. The reason for this is that we are able to look further with the eye of the imagination than at that which we see before us. The believer sees God active and present in our given, visible reality. Deeper layers of inner life are reached through the imagination than through rationality.[2]

This sort of imagination has nothing to do with a fantasizing that is an escape from reality. It is a pedagogic tool whereby the invisible reality may be spoken of and called forth, and as such it comes alive. As with Jesus' parables about the sower, the shepherd, the pearl, and the mustard seed, it is the way that points toward deeper insight. Jesus spoke to the multitude in images and likenesses, but he gave his disciples the more profound insight that it was about the reality of God's kingdom and the proclamation of God's Word (see Matthew 13). The liturgy of the sacraments establishes actual encounters with God in this way. Here we must also keep in mind the distinction between idol and icon. Our representations are only a means of passage to the spiritual whereby we realize that God approaches us first, and that all talk about and to the Invisible empties into silence before the mystery.

This spiritual experience is described phenomenologically as what Jean-Luc Marion calls a "saturated phenomenon" *(phénomène saturé)*. The believer experiences that divine reality rises endlessly above our own experience but also pervades our innermost depths. Karl Jaspers has already spoken about the symbol as "intensified reality" *(gesteigerte Realität)*. Our knowledge of what is really real is raised to unknown heights where we come up against the limits of our rational knowledge and humbly acknowledge that we are accepted and taken up into this higher reality rising above us. The human experience of "there is something more, something higher or deeper that carries us" leads to a surrender, the origin of faith (Kierkegaard), the letting go of certainties in order to cling to "what has been promised to us" from revelation. The Christian narrative, as interpretation of that divine mystery, ultimately remains improvable, if open to debate in the context of apologetics, but it is not inhumanly irrational to continue to have faith in it as a life narrative of the finite human being, who is situated in tradition and culture.

God's Love as Gift

The category of gift is central to the Christian interpretation of the divine mystery. The entire Christian tradition emphasizes that "God so loved the world that he *gave* his only Son, so that everyone who believes in him might not perish but might have eternal life" (John 3:16). This fundamental "given" (*Being Given*, Marion) is an undeniable fact. This category comes to the fore in a postmodern theology as a foundation and pillar of fundamental theology, of the doctrine of creation, of Christology, and of sacramental theology. In the doctrine of the Trinity, three persons given to one another in continuous mutual exchange and convergence of love *(perichorēsis)* and flowing forth *(ekporeusis, processio)* to creation in the incarnation of the Son of God in Jesus are so many "givens": voluntary, disinterested givens and gifts that, even if it should come down to it, ask for no return.

The gift is only complete and really a gift when a return is never presumed. That is the fundamental mystery of love *(agapē)*. This experience is reflected when persons (for)give one another purely out of goodness, generosity, and benevolence. There is no true gift as long as we give in order to receive something in return.

The gift is integral only when we acknowledge the surplus value or certainly the equality and the singularity of the other. The three divine persons, Father, Son, and Spirit, are continuously given to one another in a consummate unity of love. This love emanates out to creation, where the human person is called to freedom as God's representative. The Christology of the Western tradition is marked by a theory of redemption of which Anselm is an exponent with the doctrine of satisfaction *(satisfactio)*. The eternal Son of God became human as atonement for sin. Syrian patrology, on the other hand, developed the vision from Saint Ephrem, among others, that even without the fall, God wanted to complete creation in Jesus by making it a participant in the divine life.

God's self-communication to humanity in the person of Jesus, situated in time and space and shown in the paschal mystery, proceeds further in those ecclesial actions that, as sacraments, represent God's gift to us here and now.

Perspective: Beyond Obligatory Expectations

The truly Christian meaning of a sacrament comes fully into its own beginning with the vision of the sacraments as icons in which God gazes upon humanity and continuously gives himself to the faithful in the various circumstances of their lives. Stripped of an "I-give-so-that-you-might-give" mentality and an obligatory character, stripped also of a view of sacraments as a magically conceived cause of grace, the experience of the sacraments can claim its own worth in the current philosophical and cultural climate. It can do so by gratuitously and voluntarily accepting God's gift of participation in the deepest reality. It is unnecessary for God that we accept God's self-communication—the gift is disinterested—but it is up to the human person to acknowledge him- or herself to be in the position of someone to whom is given *(les adonnés)*. This means that the person does not consider him- or herself to constitute the norm in a freely chosen individualism and fraudulent subjectivism, but, rather, that he or she opens up to the Other who gives. Is this not the call to the freedom to respond consciously to God's offer in Christ and his Spirit? This is where the sacraments take their place in the life of the Christian, as ritual moments with a strongly religious flavor. As metaphorical celebrations of existence, they ask for a typically Christian interpretation as the mouthpiece, the language of God's gift.

Chapter Six

WITH THE SILENT GLIMMER OF GOD'S SPIRIT

My grace is sufficient for you.
(2 Corinthians 12:9)

To celebrate the sacraments is to enter into a dialogue with the self-giving God. We allow God's Word to come to us, and we know that Jesus' story directly addresses us. This encounter unfolds in the real circumstances of our life. It is rooted in the power of the living Spirit who issues forth from the Father and the Son. In this way, we come to stand in the mutual love of the three divine persons and become immersed, as it were, in this divine mystery. We participate in their love that is offered to us. Our response to God's love, which consists in voluntary acceptance and thankfulness, is itself possible only through the power of the Spirit active and moving within us.

Reforming the Classical View of Grace

Classical theology conceives of the effects of the sacraments in categories of grace that are communicated to the faithful. Ontologically based theology sees grace as a situation, an attitude, a condition *(habitus)*, "something" in and of the person, that a person either has or does not have, or possesses in greater or lesser degree. We need to reformulate this representation of grace, and in so doing we can be guided by the distinction made earlier between uncreated and created grace.

The term *uncreated grace* applies to the Trinity as the interpretation of their mutual exchange of love, which is transcendent, that is, above creation. This mystery of divine love is poured out on creation and, in the incarnation of Jesus, "received from the Holy Spirit." The believer is called to participate in this divine love.

Upon accepting the divine offer, the believer enters a new form of relationship with the divine persons, one indicated by the term *created grace:* the sanctifying grace in the human soul.

Renewed Understanding of Grace

In the current context of a phenomenological theology, we do well to abandon the concept of grace as a "thing" and instead to refer to grace as "God's habitation through God's Spirit." Created grace can be conceived of as a dynamic relation established by the Spirit. If we regard the sacrament as the language of the self-giving God, we direct our attention toward the gift of the Spirit. This gift is the grace of every sacrament. The Spirit is poured out in the various celebrations of the sacrament. There is no place here for an objective thinking in terms of more or less. As the third person of the Trinity, the Holy Spirit is communicated to the participants in the sacramental celebration and is also active there. The relationship that is forged between Spirit and believer is a dynamic, spiritual reality, immanent in the faithful. It is the Spirit who prays within us and who, as "the other Helper/comforter" (*paraclete;* see John 14:16 and 26), remains with the disciples after Jesus' departure. The Spirit of truth instructs these followers in the path of truth and righteousness. Therefore, the sacraments are many forms of the gift of the Spirit, God's Advocate (*advocatus)*, who strengthens us in the changing circumstances of our lives.

Spirit as Light

The greatest metaphor in all religions for the divine, transcendent mystery is light, lucidity, the clarity that bursts through and drowns the darkness.[1] The symbol of light also figures quite prominently in the Jewish and Christian traditions. It is said that God lives in inaccessible light, blinding to our eyes. The prologue to the Gospel of John, echoing the creation narrative, elaborates further on this metaphor: Jesus as "light from light."

The activity of the Holy Spirit is also represented in terms of light and fire that shine in the darkness. Blinding light is thus a symbol of the transcendent God, and participation in that divine light is described as the reflection, the splendor that shines forth from this light. The activity of the Spirit, immanent in the believer, can be characterized as a reflection of the divine light, an inner glow and warmth. The mystics bear witness to this phenomenon in their experience of the divine love (Beatrice of Nazareth, Hadewijch).

Yet, a distance from the divine also remains. We experience emptiness or a "dark night," something lacking in our senses. For that reason it is advisable to speak of the *silent glimmer* of the Holy Spirit: by this means, the human life that is sanctified by the sacraments, brought into a relation with the deepest mystery, receives a silent glimmer of divinity, a reflection and illumination of the divine life. Herein lies the uniqueness of the Christian sacraments as metaphors of daily life. The human reality that is celebrated in the sacraments receives a special luster and depth from participation in the divine life.

Both postmodernism and apophatic and negative theology are sensitive to the distinction and the difference between transcendence and immanence. The divine Other cannot simply absorb humans into itself. For that reason, participation in the divine must also maintain this distinction; but it must also confirm the connection via the mediation of language and symbols. The believer really becomes a new creation in his or her own way through God's habitation in the reception of the gift of the Spirit. He or she lives on in this mystery as a "new person." The divine is simultaneously present yet also hidden, invisible in the human form of appearance. Just as in the person of Jesus the divine came close to us and, as the Son of God, lived among us, so too the divine presence in the sacraments is also a veiled presence. The man Jesus revealed God's self most fully in his self-emptying (*kenōsis*), his not regarding "equality with God as something to be exploited" (Phil 2:6). The mystery of the incarnation of God's Son continues in the sacraments of the church. They are the ways in which the glorified humanity of Jesus *(humanitas Christi)* appears. They share in the same veiling of divinity as occurred with the man Jesus. Sacraments are human acts in which a faithful response is given to God's self-communication in Christ through the Spirit. Thus they fit into the pattern of God's self-revelation in Jesus. In this way, Jesus is again present, through the power of the Spirit, in the lives of the faithful, under the figure of human signs and speech-acts, but also illuminated from within by divinity. This divinity can be seen only by the inner eye; it can be experienced only from this inner connection, with reverence and thankfulness. For that reason, we speak of the *silent glimmer* of the Holy Spirit.

The Activity of the Sacraments

Compared to the classical interpretation of the doctrine of grace, does the theme of "the silent glimmer of God's Spirit" say enough about the activity of the sacraments? Is this characterization of the effect of the sacraments on the faithful too modest or too weak? I do not think so. My explanation of this is guided by the thought of Karl Rahner and Piet Fransen on created grace, as well as that of Jean-Luc Marion on the phenomenology of love *(charité)*.

Grace as Gift of Love

The Greek word for grace in the Bible is *charis*, the love from God to us, undeserved and unselfishly communicated.[2] It comes first, before any achievement or title of esteem. The love in return that the individual exhibits in his or her *caritas* is itself a result of this divine acceptance. Interestingly, the great scholastics never overlooked this personal character of God's love. In fact, Peter Lombard did not hesitate to compare this *caritas* with the Holy Spirit. In this vein, it is not the "Godhead" that lives within us, but rather the three distinct persons of the Trinity.

The Father lives within us as origin and source of all divinity, the first beginning and the last end, the Alpha and the Omega. The Son lives within us as the image of the Father, and thus precisely as the original image of all that is created, that is reborn in grace. That "being-image" *(eikoon)* of the Son and our own "image-of" are not static qualities. We share in the Son's life, *ut servi in Servo et ut filii in Filio* ("as servants in the Servant and as sons and daughters in the Son") through helpful obedience and filial love, because we love the world and live for it through him. As the final doxology of the Eucharistic Prayer intones, we are "through him, with him, and in him" bound in thanksgiving to the Father. The Holy Spirit resides within us because the Spirit, both within and outside of the Trinity, is the one through whom everything comes to perfection—the divine persons as well as creation (according to the mystic Ruysbroec)—each in its own way. This bringing to perfection is no static construction but the actualization of the image *(eikoon)* of the Son in us, in the dialectical tension between our external acts and our internal introspection. Put somewhat differently, the Spirit is that which propels us toward the world and toward humanity in the multiplicity of activities that form our existence, the multiplicity that develops into a living witness precisely through this "inspiration." The Spirit is also the one who allows us to rest inwardly in God, who directs our lives toward greater intimacy and unites us with God through our "heart," the most profound core of our personhood, according to the mystics. We are attached and bound to God as to the deepest ground of ourselves. God knows our "heart" and is far greater than our heart. This interior dynamic forms the rich, overflowing life of grace, a life that is not to be conceived of as a static acquisition but that bubbles up within us as a continuously renewed source of joy and fulfillment. We are immersed in that stream of grace.

Rahner's Prevenient and Accepted Grace

Karl Rahner's distinction between prevenient grace and accepted grace offers further clarification. In the first place, grace is a selfless offer *(Vorgegebenheit)* intrinsic to the divine invitation from the divine ground within us. It is a creative given-ness that gives rise to situations within which, in the context of this divine presence, the acceptance and assent to human freedom follow, and thus it becomes accepted grace. It is offered grace *(gratia oblata)* as well as accepted grace *(gratia accepta)*, both on the level of one's personal fundamental option (sanctifying grace), and on the level of the freedom of choice that develops in time and is thus called immediate grace.

Rahner regards this accepted grace not as the receptive person's own achievement, but rather as the believer's response, borne by God, who now comes to stand in the one grace, the one Love. Only those who exclude themselves from this proffered grace by means of a guilty "no" place themselves (temporarily) outside of this offer. God always reaches out to humans in self-communication.

This problem arose again in the Jansenist controversy. A distinction was made between accepted grace and purely sufficient grace (*zureichende Gnadenhilfe*), which is not active in and of itself but is elevated to the status of active grace only by human freedom. This sufficient grace was described as proportionate to the goal to be attained or dependent on the state of the recipient. Human freedom remains clearly respected, but it remains just as much an experience of faith that even this freedom is borne by grace. This is why a more adequate definition of grace is "the light of faith," clarification and inspiration by God's Spirit. The human person gains further insight into his or her faith, as well as further acceptance, by the dwelling of God's Spirit within.

A Perspective

According to Piet Fransen and Karl Rahner, the distinction between prevenient grace and its existential acceptance is as old as the theology of grace itself. Fransen pointed out a similar distinction in the work of the great Lowland mystic Jan Ruysbroec, namely, the distinction between "image" and "likeness." As told in Genesis, humans were created in the image and likeness of God. This subtle distinction regards image (*eikoon, imago*) as a quality or a property put in the person in God's name that remains undeniably present. Meanwhile, likeness (*omoioma, similitudo*) is a goal that the person attempts to realize by living in accordance with his or her deepest and final destiny.

The theology of creation and redemption has developed this theme of the *imago Dei* through the irreplaceable responsibility of the human person for the entirety of creation and a society worthy of human occupation. The theology of the sacraments connects this theme to the elaboration, activity, and fruitfulness of sacramental experience, in which the faithful participate in divine life for the life of the world (*pro mundi vita*, Jean-Luc Marion). In this perspective, the grace of the sacraments is nothing other than the Spirit, who is once again creatively active in the world.

This is a Spirit of pure love *(charis)* which, having been given beforehand (*étant donné*, Jean-Luc Marion), inspires and illumines the believer. In this mystery of gratuitous love, returning this love is no requirement for existence. Love is offered to and respects the freedom of the individual. When the offer is accepted, the self-communication is raised to a sacramental occasion whereby the participants are taken up in divine love. Gratitude and thanksgiving are the only adequate responses to the completely gratuitous love bestowed on us through the Spirit of God. In this gracious response, our lives are illuminated with an inner glow, filled with divine light that imparts a silent glimmer to daily existence. The celebrations of the seven sacraments are high points in which this glimmer breaks through in the various situations of our concrete journey through life.

Chapter Seven

BAPTISM, CONFIRMATION, EUCHARIST: SACRAMENTS OF CHRISTIAN INITIATION

The seven sacraments can be grouped according to the nature of their relationship to different life situations. Thus, the three sacraments of Christian initiation may be delineated first: baptism, confirmation, and Eucharist. They are inaugurations into the paschal mystery of Christ via reception into the ecclesial community, the foundational sacrament of the encounter with God. The sacraments of initiation accompany positive experiences in life: the wonder of being born and growing up, forming a community, and experiencing union.

Two sacraments are linked with the negative experiences of our existence, the experiences of sin, brokenness, and finitude. Here, too, in the sacraments of reconciliation and anointing of the sick, the church comes to meet the faithful by accompanying them in repentance and in the journey toward eternal life. Finally, there are two sacraments that seal an adult commitment of the faithful and empower their call before God: marriage and holy orders.

Already it is clear that the sacraments embrace the web of life. A network of symbolic acts is laid over the entirety of existence. The sacraments form a symbolic order in which the changing experiences of existence are elevated, as metaphors, to become bearers of the divine love in the Spirit.

Baptism

Initiation has existed from the very beginning of the Christian tradition. Already the Pentecost event witnessed the baptism of adults who converted to Christ after entering into the proclamation of the paschal mystery.[1] Of course this baptism, as we know it from the Acts of the Apostles, is a seal of personal conversion whereby the believer joins Jesus' disciples in their faith in the resurrection. "[Peter said] to them, 'Repent and be baptized every one of you in the name of Jesus Christ so that your sins may be forgiven; and you will receive the gift of the Holy Spirit" (Acts 2:38). It is obviously a baptism in the power of the Spirit. Whoever is filled with the Holy Spirit, whoever accepts the truth about Jesus through the word of the apostles, is baptized and taken up into Christ's mystery of death and resurrection.

Dying with Christ to the old person and being reborn to new life in the light are themes from the young church's first proclamation. A well-known ritual with water, baptism became almost self-evidently employed in the Christian community as a rite of initiation and as a way of expressing the transition from one's former life to an entirely new situation. Supported by the general human symbolism of water, namely, that of cleansing and life-giving power, the ritual of immersion in or sprinkling with water was already known both in Judaism and in the surrounding Hellenistic culture where Christianity found its origins. Thus, the ritual is not new, but the significance is: individuals are baptized "in the Name of the Lord Jesus for the forgiveness of sins." Christian baptism is clarified, on the one hand, by its connection with the earlier, familiar ritual of John the Baptist, who called all of Israel to a one-time conversion before the final judgment, which was close at hand (eschatological context), and, on the other, through its christological reference. Through baptism "in the Name of Jesus Christ" the recipient is ushered into the salvation and the redemption that have been established through Jesus.[2]

Belgian theologian Adelbert Denaux clarifies further the meaning of early Christian baptism using the following four motives: (1) Baptism brings about a qualitative change in the person. This change is expressed with metaphors: rebirth and illumination, a transition from a former, sinful life to a new, pious life. (2) Baptism is purification, a forgiving of sins. (3) Baptism brings the gift of God's Spirit. It is a seal. (4) Baptism is incorporation into the community of salvation, in the body of Christ. Baptism therefore possesses a constitutive communal dimension: this can already be appreciated in the societal model of that early Christian apostolic age when it was self-evident that when the *pater familias*, or head of the family, converted, the entire household went over to the new religion and the children were baptized as well.

The catechumenate developed in the young ecclesial community as a lengthy process of initiation with the celebration of baptism during the Easter vigil. The new Christians were then able to participate in the Easter Eucharist. This single initiation included the three sacraments of initiation that were later distinguished from one another: baptism, confirmation, and Eucharist. This remained one rite of initiation until the end of the second century and has been preserved as such in the Orthodox churches, where the celebration of infant baptism closes with the reception of holy communion by the one who has just been baptized. These churches rightly call upon "the old usage, as is found with certainty from the fourth century."[3] It is worth mentioning that the mystagogical catechesis about the deeper meaning of the initiation continued after the celebration of the rite of initiation.

Infant Baptism

In its further historical development, infant baptism received a place in the church as a lasting intuition of faith. From the realization that children belong in the church, the practice of infant baptism became a constant throughout its entire history. The theological justification for infant baptism is supported by the faith-filled realization that entrance into the mystery of Christ cannot be refused to children because they raise no obstacle themselves. This is a minimal threshold, however. Therefore, the parents' faith is rightly to be taken into account, as well as that of the community in which these children are to be received. Infant baptism has received enough theological argumentation in the tradition to remain justifiably alive, not as an ill-considered generalization (just baptize because of tradition or folklore) but on the basis of the

44

parents' conscious decision on behalf of their child. Moreover, in the current context, the requirements of faith motivation for infant baptism have been strengthened. Each request for baptism must be gauged according to the deeper attitude of faith of the environment in which the child will grow up, and assurances of further Christian upbringing will be required.

Infant Baptism and Postmodernity

In the context of a postmodern vision of the sacraments, the practice of infant baptism can be defined further in the categories of the gratuitous gift of God's Spirit. The self-communication of God in Christ through the Spirit is a sign of God's "first" love, which is communicated in ecclesial activity. Here, the anthropological context is one of pure receptivity, gratitude at the reception of new life, realization that this new life has been granted to us. Baptism is also a present, a gift of God expressed in human language and symbol: with the naming "for God and the human community," the confession of faith in the child's name, the rite with the baptismal water as a symbol of new birth, the anointing to conformity with Christ in the power of the Spirit, the gift of light in the baptismal candle, the white cloth....

In this manner, the act of baptism is a speech-act in which the meaning of Christ is actualized for this child in this concrete community. The liturgical celebration is a meaningful symbolic act, where what is said really happens to the child and the community that is present. This language is performative; it does what it says. The gift of the Spirit really takes place. The child effectively becomes a "child of God," a child of the Light, through this sacrament. He or she is taken up, by means of the ecclesial act, in the community of salvation of the church, as the continuation of the "body of Christ."

Human reality comes to its fullest appearance in the sacramental celebration, with the glimmer of divine illumination. That which this human reality already contains in and of itself—gratitude for the wonder of new life—is now transposed, transferred (in the metaphor) to the deepest meaning of this life. We celebrate the mystery of our faith in the visible order. In this way, baptism is the *first* sacrament of faith. Our faith becomes effective in language and signs with regard to and for this child. We celebrate that this child is also a child of God, that he or she receives a redemptive portion in Christ's paschal mystery, that he or she is a new creation in the Spirit, reborn from water and the Holy Spirit.

Baptism grants to the child a real status as a baptized person within the community. Initiation has to do with the transition from a former condition to a new status. This occurs in infant baptism, certainly in the full receptivity of the child. But this is the normal human condition of every human child who will grow up in a community. For this very reason, infant baptism is the *sacrament of the beginning*. It is the gateway *(janua)* of the symbolic order of the sacraments. In the visible order where the sacraments interpret the language of the self-giving God, this sacrament may be regarded as fully worthy within its own contours. Infant baptism imparts its own status to these human beings within the ecclesial community. It is the foundation of the other sacraments, and it is recalled at so many later moments in life.

Infant baptism places this person once and for all in relation to the Trinity, with the presence of God within, as "baptized" in the church. This grants the person an undeniable identity and particularity (what was meant classically by the *character* of the sacrament), a participation in the mystery of Christ that cannot be undone. The person receives a definitive, eschatological destiny. In anticipation of his or her ultimate destination, this person is called to union with God, through the act within the church, and he or she belongs to God's chosen ones. This is confessed in faith and invoked in hope in the liturgy of infant baptism.

The Impact of Baptism

Without describing the effects of this baptism in metaphysical terms, the irreplaceable worth of this symbolic act at the beginning of life can also be clarified from a psycho-philosophical angle. Jean-Marie Jaspard arrives at the following conclusion in his epistemological analysis of the ritual of baptism as symbolic act:

That a newborn is the central figure and the one favored most importantly in the baptismal rite is doubtless a valid observation. The rite will function symbolically on several levels, provided that a few conditions are present. In accordance with the parents' will, it will signify the child's entrance into the Catholic Church, out of pure tradition or to admit the child to the living network of relations of such a community. The newborn is, as such, able to take part in the relationships mediated by his or her parents. In that sense the infant is open to a relationship with God, as long as his or her parents do not exclude him or her from their own religious observances and they give concrete expression to their convictions. Baptism, together with all the rites that compose it, can give expression to their meaning most fully as rites of passage or initiation in a life of faith that the child experiences, first as handed on by his or her parents, before the child is capable of assuming this personally in a free and independent manner.[4]

Confirmation: A Historical Overview

In the Western church, the single initiation is spread out in separate celebrations. In the North African churches from the third century on, the last of the postbaptismal anointings was reserved for the bishop, who confirmed *(confirmatio)* in a separate ceremony the baptism that had been administered in local churches by priests or deacons. The second sacrament of initiation came into being from this practice. It became known by the name *confirmation.* In the twelfth century it was taken up into systematic reflection on the seven sacraments. In this way, a distinction came into existence between baptism with the cleansing from sin and rebirth, and the anointing with the power of the Spirit. The separation of these two core elements of the one ritual of initiation is of a purely ecclesial and institutional nature.[5]

Transitional Period

In the transitional period from late antiquity to the early Middle Ages, the baptism of small children became increasingly the general practice. In the emerging liturgy of infant baptism the formerly separate catechumenal ceremonies for adults were reduced to a unified form for a single occasion. The contraction of the various catechumenal celebrations into the one (infant) baptism had a negative consequence for the isolation of the second core element in the Western tradition's single initiation. As Jozef Lamberts correctly observes, "The result for the second sacrament of initiation was that its administration went without ritual preparation and remained relatively poor in prayer texts and signs for more than a thousand years."[6] It is indeed the case that the administration of confirmation—we can hardly speak of "celebration" for this entire period—occurred when the children were brought to the bishop or when the bishop visited the parishes.[7]

History shows that confirmation was not to be delayed for too long after baptism, and that, as a rule, it had to have taken place before the children were admitted to the Eucharist. This occurred when they could distinguish between regular bread and wine and the body and blood of Christ—the "years of discretion" that were situated between the ages of seven and twelve. The order of the sacraments of initiation as baptism, confirmation, Eucharist was altered in 1910 when Pope Pius X moved children's communion forward to the age of seven. Confirmation was administered in many countries around the age of twelve and therefore after first Eucharist.

Scholastic Synthesis

In the scholastic synthesis, confirmation receives a separate place between the "greater" sacraments (*sacramenta maiora*), that is, baptism and Eucharist. It is difficult, however, to define the uniqueness of confirmation. In fact, it is nothing other than the confirmation of baptism by means of the final anointing performed by the bishop. As sacrament it imparts "an increase of grace," a gift of the Spirit for the strengthening of faith in order to witness to the faith. Thomas Aquinas's typification of confirmation as the sacrament of the fulfilled age *(aetas perfecta)* was intended to express that the recipient of this sacrament was spiritually eligible to receive the Eucharist, but later this was interpreted to mean adulthood. The theme of the strength or power *(robur)* communicated by this second sacrament was also interpreted in terms of fitness for service and chivalrous zeal for apostleship. In comparison with infant baptism, which is represented as spiritual rebirth *(generatio)* in Christ, we see in confirmation a certain spiritual augmentation *(quoddam spirituale augmentum)*. We should be aware that, in the hermeneutics of scholastic theology, metaphysics (thought at the level of ontology) ought not to be confused with psychological growth.

The Views of the Reformers

The magisterial Reformers Luther, Calvin, and Zwingli deny that confirmation is one of the sacraments instituted by Christ (from the principle of *sola scriptura*). They also object to a too magical administration of this sacrament by the bishop, who would impart grace (in conflict with the principle of *sola gratia*). They do, however, emphasize the personal confession of faith that children can make when they have received the proper preparation that enables them to do so (the *sola fide* principle). This can be appreciated in their reorganization of the catechism lessons, which were begun in the churches of the Reformation and later followed in the Catholic Reformation with the Tridentine catechism and the small catechisms of the dioceses.

In place of confirmation, the Protestant churches hold a ceremony whereby young people make a solemn statement of their confession of faith as a remembrance of and personal confirmation of their infant baptism. In the Calvinistic churches this confession of faith is a requirement for admission to the Lord's Supper. The development within the Catholic Church, where more and more use of the catechism is made in preparation for participation in the Eucharist—though confirmation in and of itself still receives little attention—can be interpreted as an exponent of modernity, where the attention goes to the subject and to rationality. In my estimation, the question of placing confirmation at an older age is also to be interpreted as having arisen from the "modern" mind-set. Although the reasons for an older age are very worthy of consideration, especially from the perspective of pastoral solicitude, scholars of liturgy and ecumenically minded theologians raise objections with regard to the inversion of the order in the single process of initiation and the excessive separation of infant baptism and confirmation. The Second Vatican Council placed the initiating character of confirmation in the limelight without imposing a definite age. The bishops' conferences retained the freedom to determine which solution was best in their estimation.

Currently there is a serious consideration of all the motives, theological, liturgical, ecumenical, as well as pastoral. In his hermeneutics of history, Henri Bourgeois has shown the correctness of the claims of the various traditions within the sacramental economy of salvation and appreciates the legitimate plurality in the usages of the church. Yet the unity of the sacraments of initiation remains a guiding principle for theological reflection for him as well. In Bourgeois' estimation, it is essential that the difference between baptism and confirmation should not be made rigid: the Eastern church has never given in to that temptation, whereas the Western church has not always avoided it. In order to arrive at responsible and mutually acceptable insights and practices, Bourgeois believes that the Western churches are called to pastoral imagination, ecumenical attention, and theological courage.[8]

Confirmation in a Postmodern Context

How can postmodern reflection bring some clarity to this? As we have seen, we have become more aware of the irresponsibility of our speech and thought about God after the end of the grand meta-narratives. Postmodern theology is reluctant even to affirm the presence of God and Christ in the sacred signs. Rather, the accent lies on the symbolic character of the celebrations, in which the distance as well as the proximity of the divine is expressed. And, as is typical in postmodern sacramental theology, there is the turn from the subject to the broader community. The individual person can make his or her own choices "à la carte" and, at first sight, independently. Still, such an individualistic subjectivism is unmasked in this way, because the individual seems to be more dependent than ever on manipulation and social structures.

In view of the above, the celebration of confirmation can be clarified as the second step in Christian initiation, as *a guidance in growth* toward adulthood in Christianity. In our current time, pastoral ministry devotes much attention to a suitable confession of faith and the catechesis of young people. The celebration of confirmation is a nodal point around which serious initiatives are taken in all parishes to allow this occasion to develop to a real ecclesial experience.

In this perspective, the role of the community is highlighted in a postmodern reflection on this sacrament—not the old community, which would merely perpetuate former traditions, but rather the community that attains a worthy configuration within which individuals can identify themselves. On that point, the great rituals of life are the medium by which the postmodern person relates to the divine, the transcendent mystery, out of anthropological necessity and in a secularized culture. Certain sociologists have explained that this phenomenon is the most tenacious remnant of the religious forms of society. But there is also an alternative explanation—that it is really about something "eternally human" that finds expression in a ritual in which the person discerns the proximity of the divine. The purely rationalistic concept that a person disposes of him- or herself in total freedom yields to awareness that the person is identified in a broader context transmitted by values acknowledged within this subgroup. The rituals of initiation stand precisely in this tradition as the most important means of giving a person a Christian identity, by accepting the person into the community and allowing him or her to participate in the values and convictions that are alive in it.

In this way, confirmation is a real sacrament of initiation: initiation in the faith at the threshold of young adulthood and being brought further into the church by parents, companions, catechists, and pastors. The parents who, within their Christian marriage, give their children a faith-filled upbringing as they promised at the time of baptism, and who exemplify Christian life in word and deed, make various choices for their children. At first totally, and gradually more and more together with the children, they make choices in the growth of this life of faith and being church. In this way, in choosing first communion and, later, confirmation for their child, they are expressing their firm intention for the Christian development of their family, an ecclesial condensation of the option for Christian life. The scale of guidance broadens to the parish, with attention to the larger ecclesial community.

Confirmation and the Gift of the Spirit

If baptism is the sacrament of the beginning, confirmation is the *sacrament of growth*. Indeed, this sacrament is a gift at the same time, a renewed gift of the Spirit in the circumstances of growth in the Christian community. Confirmation has been unjustly represented as the sacrament that alone confers the gift of the Spirit, as if baptism did not yet contain any gift of the Spirit. With the growth in Christian life and in the greater connection with the ecclesial community, this gift of the Holy Spirit is to be interpreted as both relational and dynamic, not as a static reality. It is a gift of the Spirit that propels one toward greater involvement and mutual love, toward more profound knowledge and witness. It is correct to connect the gifts of the Spirit at Pentecost with this sacrament, as we also acknowledge these gifts by each of the other sacraments. The central text of this sacrament is: "N., be sealed with the gift of the Holy Spirit."

The baptized person is spoken to anew by name in his or her particularity and uniqueness. The "seal" *(sfragis)* points to the seal, confirmation of the baptism, as the gift of God. It is a renewed gift of the Holy Spirit, only now in the circumstances of development toward adulthood. Clearly, the character of gift is central to a postmodern theology: the sacrament as the language of the self-giving God. This central formulation is its most simple expression.

Age of Confirmation and Pastoral Discernment

In postmodern reflection, with its attention to the structural symbolic coherence of the rituals and the diminution of instrumental/subject-focused rationality, this sacrament will be regarded as the second step in a single process of initiation. At a moment in the life of the individual, the church community celebrates the sacrament of confirmation. This sacrament effects the recipient's greater involvement with the community. Here too, the individual's receptivity is valued more highly than his or her active involvement in the church. At the time of confirmation, the receptivity is supposed to be at the level of the developing child. Later, the individual will increasingly be called upon to be actively and responsibly engaged in the sacraments that frame human life, whether Eucharist, marriage, and/or holy orders. We "are" baptized and confirmed. We receive these sacraments of initiation from the surrounding community. Initiation also means to receive and confer one's own status. The *confirmandi* receive their status within the church as "confirmed." Their baptism is now confirmed and personalized, partly through themselves and at the appropriate level of their growth in the community. The meaning of being a baptized and confirmed Christian takes on more content for them through continuing catechesis and guidance in faith.

When the child grows further in a network of meanings and narratives, it is vitally important that this first initiation be carried over into the domestic and parochial circle. "In this context, there can only be talk of confirmation at the youngest age, of a ritual celebration and anointing, when a religious community exists, prepares the initiation and aims at an orientation of life that is concurrently integrated in daily life and that is not subordinated to rationalistic ideology."[9] This is the task of the initiating community, which accepts new members into its midst and helps them grow up to become adult, conscious Christians. Pastoral options play a role in the evolution of a broad church of the people into an ecclesial community of conscious, engaged Christians. For these, confirmation at a later age is frequently a better expression of their faith convictions and the firm will to behave as Christians. In the future it is possible that confirmation will more likely be celebrated at the time of young adulthood, although this depends on decisions of the respective Bishops' Conferences. It is delightful to see how young adults, and adults who were not confirmed as children, experience this sacrament with great conviction and admirable honesty.

What is at stake here is the challenge of making confirmation a real sacrament of faith and not merely a rite of passage. This is a challenge that faces the church leadership for the future.

It is not possible to change a tradition suddenly and quickly. We must remain attentive to the signs of the current times in the experience of the ecclesial community in order, with good leadership, effectively to realize an authentic experience of faith in the sacrament. The following description can serve as an open working definition:

> Situated in the journey of children or youth on the way to an adult faith, the celebration of confirmation represents the expression and consolidation of fellowship in the church through the profession of faith on the part of the young people, and on the part of the church the recognition of a special gift of the Spirit in the midst of a local church community under the leadership of a bishop who presides at the ceremony or is represented by a delegated priest. Those to be confirmed are called again by their name, more bonded to Christ and equipped with a renewed gift of the Spirit for witness, greater spiritual depth, and the building up of the Church.[10]

Eucharist

The celebration of the Eucharist stands as the completion of Christian initiation, and it is the greatest and most important sacrament. The inauguration into the mystery of Christ achieves its fullest expression in the memorial celebration of Jesus' death and resurrection. This is the sacrament in which God's gift, together with the Holy Spirit, is communicated again and again in the various circumstances in which the sacrament is celebrated. In uniting with Jesus' acts during the Last Supper with his disciples, the ecclesial community actualizes, in the celebration of the Eucharist, the full meaning of this prophetic gift of his body and blood.

Jesus' Real Eucharistic Presence

Jesus is really present in the gifts of bread and wine through the power of the Spirit in the actions of the church. Throughout the entire history of the Christian community, believers have claimed that Jesus is present in a special way in this sacrament. Theological reflection has offered various explanations for this unique kind of real presence. In antiquity it was based primarily on a Neoplatonic vision of the symbol; in scholasticism it resulted from the application of Aristotelian epistemological concepts such as substance and accident. The miraculous transformation of bread and wine into the body and blood of Jesus remained ultimately inscrutable here as well. Thomas Aquinas points out that in the miracle of the eucharistic consecration human understanding must be helped by faith.

The Classical Attempt to Explain Real Presence

As a theological interpretation, "transubstantiation" became the most obvious term to make this miracle accessible at the level of rational knowledge. Here Aristotelian concepts are employed so that "substance" means what something actually "is," and "accidents" are the principles of attending aspects, such as how something looks. We still see bread and wine as characteristic features of the accidents, but the most profound reality is no longer bread and wine, but rather the body and blood on the basis of substance. We should be careful to note that an operation is carried out that is the radical opposite of what was expressed in Aristotelian epistemology. In Aristotelian epistemology, the principle of substance exists as the foundation even if the outward appearance of this substance can change on the basis of the accidents. The miraculous transformation in the Eucharist occurs on the basis of the new substance of Jesus' body and blood, which takes the place of the substance of bread and wine. From a philosophical perspective, we are deviating completely from a strict metaphysics, where it is unthinkable that the substance can exist independently of the accidents and where the transformation always happens on the basis of the accidents. It is for that reason that the church did not retain the term *accidents*, but does use "the species" *(species)*, the outward appearance. The acknowledgment of the real presence of Jesus under the species of bread and wine still requires a surrender to faith. It cannot be explained philosophically, not even with the help of Aristotelian terms from a metaphysical and ontological perspective.

Other Attempts to Explain Presence

Other explanations from symbolic thinking acknowledge the shift in meaning: the most profound significance of the consecrated bread and wine is no longer the reality of bread and wine. The body and blood are now the deepest reality and the ultimate destination of these earthly realities. These modern explanations were indeed recognized in the official doctrine of the church, on the basis of a symbolic character that is removed from ontological terminology. They were considered to be good approaches to a correct insight into the real presence, but they were still regarded as an inadequate means of indicating the miraculous transformation. The term *transubstantiation* was still regarded as the most appropriate description and elucidation, even though it is not dogmatically obligatory.

Real Presence and Postmodernity

A postmodern approach also distances itself from the ontological terminology of substance and accidents. Phenomenology reflects resolutely upon the gift-character of the symbolic acts that Jesus performed at the Last Supper. His self-giving is total. In the words of consecration, "This is my body" and "This is…the blood of the new and everlasting covenant," a performative language is spoken that realizes what is said. The language generates anew the intended meaning.

Jesus gives his life. He gives his body as shared bread and wine marked with a unique significance, that is, his ultimate gift of self. This meaning is realized anew in the ecclesial act for the participants in the eucharistic gathering. They share in his self-gift of his body and blood, by eating this bread and drinking this wine. In this way they realize the greatest possible union with Jesus. The gift is there, even if it is not received. The real presence does not depend on the acceptance or acknowledgment of the faithful, but is realized from the acts of Jesus himself, continued in the ecclesial rite.

In his reflections on the Eucharist, Jean-Luc Marion emphasizes this objective character of Jesus' self-offering, independent of
human approval.[11] The real presence is the fruit of God's acting in
Jesus, summoned again in the Eucharistic prayer of the church.

Interestingly, a postmodern approach emphasizes more
strongly than before the faith-filled community that celebrates the
Eucharist together, participating in Jesus' self-offering in the
speech-act and with the symbols of bread and wine. The central
part of the Eucharist consists of the prayer of thanksgiving in which
the Holy Spirit is invoked twice *(epiclesis):* once over the gifts of
bread and wine, and once over the gathered community.

The Power of the Spirit

When we reflect further on this supplication to the Holy
Spirit that the Spirit transform the gifts into the body and blood of
Jesus and the gathered community into one body of Christ, we can
leave behind the ontological categories and categorically describe
the eucharistic event as an action of the church in the power of the
Spirit. It is the Creator Spirit *(creator Spiritus)* who transforms both
the gifts and our very selves into the body of Christ. The sacrament, as the language of the self-giving God in the Holy Spirit,
ensures that this gift is really present again and realizes most fully
the deepest meaning of Jesus' self-giving in the Spirit.

The faithful are united with this gift in the power of the Spirit,
taken up in the stream of divine love, participants in the fruit of
redemption. They gratefully acknowledge the unselfish gift of God
and become real participants in divine life through communion.
The divine Word is creative: it determines most profoundly what
bread and wine mean and "are," and what we believers "are" as the
people of God and body of Christ in the power of the Holy Spirit.
Is not the deepest transformation in reality expressed in this way?
By placing ourselves in the dynamic of God's gift, we realize union
(communio) in the divine mystery of Love.

Therefore, the Eucharist is regarded in the first place as a gift
of the Spirit to the church. The attention is not so much on what
we say and do as on the loving self-communication of God's Spirit,

who allows us to share anew "in the silent glimmer" of God's image and likeness.

Eucharist and Life

The Eucharist is celebrated in the various circumstances of life as a sign of the end times, an anticipation of the definitive union with God. We bring our daily life along in every eucharistic celebration in order to unite it with Jesus' self-giving, for we know that our circumstances are open to full redemption through Jesus. Our little narrative as human beings is laid upon the pattern of Jesus' narrative in which God reveals himself and where the Spirit is continuously active. Thus, besides the central actions of the Eucharistic prayer and communion, there is also the Liturgy of the Word, in which the Gospel always actualizes a fragment of Jesus' preaching. Here, too, Jesus is present again in the power of the Spirit, "who reminds us of everything about Jesus" and makes us into Jesus' contemporaries. His word is now directed at us so that we might model our lives on his narrative.

Since the Second Vatican Council, extensive attention has been paid to the renewed constitution of the Lectionary with a better distribution of biblical texts over the cycle of the liturgical year. At the same time, we should point out that being addressed by the word of Jesus is once more a gift of the Spirit, who makes us attentive and opens our hearts to the biblical message.

The Eucharist: Summit of Christian Initiation

The Eucharist is the high point of Christian initiation and acknowledgment of our identity as the people of God by following Christ in the power of the Spirit. At the same time, the celebration in remembrance of Jesus' suffering and resurrection is an anticipation of the coming fullness of God's kingdom. This kingdom of God has come into our midst in Jesus, and it aspires to its completion at the end of time. This eschatological direction imparts a joyful character to the celebration in the interim, in the conviction of the ultimate, full union with God in Christ and the Spirit. Until that happens, the Eucharist is celebrated "until he comes again" as a proclamation of God's Word. The celebration of remembrance of Jesus' self-offering in time takes the shape of a banquet celebration in anticipation of the heavenly "Lord's Banquet," the feast upon the mountain that attracts all peoples. It is spiritual food for the journey. Here too, the glimmer of divine life is still veiled and silent. We are on the way to the fullness of union with God. Human pain and suffering, division and discord are still our lot. The Eucharist has been established as a sign for the peoples of the "notwithstanding-all-that" of this situation. Despite pain and division, the Eucharist can still be celebrated as a silent protest, a "silent scream," as Dorothee Sölle puts it, against the injustice and impotence that still afflict our world and not only are the result of the rejection of God's love, but also seem to be the fate of the mortal human being.

The Eucharist is a sign of hope against injustice and a sign of the faith of those who trust in God. It is a sign of peace in the middle of injustice and division in expectation "until he comes again," not just projected in a temporal vacuum upon a vague future, but as a present certainty and security in God's love. This is also a fruit of God's gift in the Eucharist.

The Eucharist remains the central celebration of the paschal mystery in Christian life, the measure of Christian identity. Leon Lemmens has described profoundly the meaning of this sacrament as Jesus' costly parting gift to his disciples, in which the bond between them is always experienced anew in friendship. "Through the gift of the Holy Spirit, they make their own the religious conviction that Jesus Christ inspired and they can gradually become an icon of the Father's love."[12]

The *epiclesis* in the fifth Eucharistic prayer (one of several "extra" Eucharistic prayers permitted in the Low Countries) gives voice to this:

Father, send now the Comforter and Helper to our midst, your Holy Spirit.
Awaken the conviction of Jesus Christ in our hearts.
Strengthen our trust, increase our love.
Touch us with the fire of your Spirit
and bring us closer to one another

Lemmens also cites another special Eucharistic prayer from the Low Countries, the eleventh:

Merciful God, let the Spirit of Jesus live within us
and fill us with your love.
Strengthen us through the gifts of his body and blood
and make us into new people;
that we may resemble Jesus.

He concludes: "The life of Christians and the Christian community grow together with the life of Jesus and become a gift to the Father. Thanks to the Holy Spirit, they are able to sanctify his Name and become servants of his friendship among people."[13] Bishop Paul Schruers has also pointed out the role of the Holy Spirit in the establishment of the ecclesial *communio:* "The Holy Spirit, gift of the Son, is, according to Paul (2 Cor 13:13) the one who realizes the communion. He does not awaken each individual, separated Christian, but rather the faithful who always stand in relation to one another in a history of *communio.*"[14] The Eucharist builds up the ecclesial community. "The model and source of the *communio* is the love between Father and Son in the Holy Spirit. God's love circulates thusly in the community, in the unity in diversity, in mutual love. The Holy Spirit always brings the community together again by actualizing the words of Jesus in always new circumstances. This gathering into a community happens in a special manner in the spiritual gifts that are the sacraments of baptism and Eucharist. In this way, the community can live in Jesus, remaining in His word and His love."[15]

Chapter Eight

RECONCILIATION AND ANOINTING: SACRAMENTS OF HEALING

This chapter will examine the sacraments of reconciliation (formerly known as confession) and anointing of the sick (formerly extreme unction). These sacraments can be brought together as sacraments of healing in the anthropological context of the brokenness of human existence. They address negative life experiences of failure, suffering, and finitude.

The symbolic network of sacraments that spans all of life does not avoid its negative aspects. The sacraments are given "for healing and salvation," not in the sense that they abolish failure or finitude, but rather in the sense that they offer a view of how Christian life addresses these experiences of finitude. Jesus forgave many sinners during his life, and he went through the darkness of suffering and death himself. The sacraments of the church set forth these facets of Jesus' life and death. The hands of Jesus, reaching out to sinners and spread open upon the wood of the cross, minister to sinful, suffering, and dying people by means of these ecclesial acts.

The Sacrament of Reconciliation

The history of the sacrament of reconciliation has been dotted with various crises. In each instance, it underwent reform and renewal of its forms of expression for Christians who want to reconcile with God within the context of the ecclesial community.[1] Within this process of alteration and reform, a point of continuity persisted. There is a kernel of truth and specificity in the act of reconciliation that will be a constant in its future form of expression. In that sense, there is an open tradition under the inspiration of the

Holy Spirit, wherein continuity with the past as well as creativity in an eschatological perspective are both operative. In Paul Ricoeur's hermeneutical terms, a certain "figure" is identifiable in the act of reconciliation, prefigured *(préfiguré)* in fundamental patterns from the biblical message and history. These form the basis for a new figure for our contemporary thought-world *(configuration)* that fulfills the real intention of this sacrament, namely, the conversion and reconciliation of the faithful *(réfiguration)*.

Is a New Age Dawning?

Given the dimensions of the crisis in which the practice of sacramental reconciliation now finds itself, we may well ask whether we, in this postmodern era, stand at the threshold of a renewed experience of reconciliation by means of ecclesial intercession. Can we speak of a new period in the history of this sacrament?

Delineating periods in history depends upon a shift in accent or paradigm, indicators of the experience of this sacrament. Three periods are distinguished in practically all surveys of history: the regime of the unrepeatable *canonical penance*, from antiquity until the sixth century; the repeatable, milder *tariff penance*, a system that was spread across the continent by Irish/Celtic monks beginning in the seventh century; and the sacrament of penance *(sacramentum poenitentiae)*, the form of expression from the middle of the twelfth century until the Second Vatican Council, which occurred particularly in the form of individual confession. Nowadays, we may rightly wonder whether or not we find ourselves in a period of transition to a fourth period in the form and experience of this sacrament, one that, in the post–Vatican II era, is more properly called the sacrament of reconciliation *(reconciliatio)*.[2] The division into these periods is based on theological reflection on the act of reconciliation. As far as the form of expression is concerned, it could be said that there are only two periods, the period of canonical (public) penance that occurred in the middle of the ecclesial community, and then, from the seventh century on, the period in which private, individual confession was the new basic pattern. Theologically, the important difference is that between 1140 and 1150 the practice of penance was acknowledged and absorbed into the seven sacraments. As a result, a better coherence was established between the various elements of repentance, confession, absolution, and atonement. In relation to the hermeneutics of this act we should not forget that up until that point the practice of penance was experienced as an ecclesial regulation, an earlier disciplinary arrangement, whereas after 1140, with the writings of Peter Lombard, sacramental efficacy came to occupy the foreground.

This demarcation of periods applies only to the developments in the Western church and theology and refers only to the ecclesial intercession of reconciliation. In addition to this form, there is room for one's personal reconciliation with God in conversion of heart, through contrition *(contritio)* and the various other forms of daily reconciliation, such as fasting, almsgiving, prayer, pilgrimages, and reconciliation with one another. Here we will deal with the specific form of expression that was acknowledged as a sacrament in scholastic theology, accepting that its previous history had taken the shape of canonical penance and tariff penance. The division into periods is legitimate because these systems followed and (partially) replaced one another. We could compare it with an above-ground pedestrian crossing on the paths of reconciliation, while an underground railway of continuity proceeds around the same basic data. At the end of the first and second periods, crises occurred that resulted in renewal and redemption. And so we repeat our question: In our postmodern age, have we not arrived at the acknowledgment of a crisis in the practice of private confession, so that a renewal is urgently needed that can be designed with the basic pattern of Scripture and tradition as reference point?

The theology of the third period analyzed the scholastic concepts in terms of Aristotelian metaphysics, which was appropriated to clarify the working of the sacrament (the "matter–form" pattern and the sacrament seen as the cause of grace). In our postmodern approach, we will view the sacrament again as the language of the self-giving God, as a renewed gift of the Holy Spirit that illuminates the inner heart of the believer, invites him or her to conversion, and offers God's reconciliation as a gratuitous gift.

New Testament Perspectives

Jesus himself forgave countless sinners and entrusted the task of reconciliation to the apostles. Initially, on the basis of the proclamation of and about the Lord Jesus, "who died for our sins," a liberal attitude was embraced vis-à-vis the sinners in the ecclesial community. The parable of the prodigal son places the unconditional conviction of the merciful Father's forgiveness before our eyes as an example to follow: to be generous as the heavenly Father is generous. Forgiveness of one another is central to the evangelical manner of life of Jesus' followers ("Not seven times, but, I tell you, [forgive] seventy-seven times" [Matt 18:22]).

Two New Testament texts in which the explicit exhortation is given to confess one's sins to one another (1 John 1:9 and James 5:16) may be regarded as the beginning of a practice in the young church community that later developed into the sacrament of penance. The sources from the first centuries are insufficient for us to reach a general conclusion concerning a binding regulation about the penance required after serious sin. There are sporadic, regional indications of a second, unrepeatable ecclesial reconciliation after baptism, which is the first sacrament of conversion.

From Liberalism to Rigorism

Tertullian (second–third centuries) and Cyprian (middle of the third century) are witnesses to a rising rigorist attitude, a strict regulation regarding penance in the Western church, although Bishop Cyprian finally opted for a liberal concession to those who lapsed during times of persecution. In contrast to the Syrian liturgy (*Didascalia*), the vision of Clement of Alexandria (beginning of the third century), and Origen (middle of the third century), in which the aspects of purification and healing are key in the act of penance, the developments in the West can be seen as a gradual increase in strictness after an initially liberal attitude toward sinners in the church. This is what seems to have happened: the line of development from New Testament times goes not from a strict rigorist to a more permissive attitude, but rather the reverse: from an originally liberal attitude to a stricter regime. It was the merit of theologians and bishops from the third century onward that they judged such rigorism to be a deviation in the tradition of penance. Instead, they emphasized God's mercy to the sinner who converted. They were able to preserve both components—a holy way of life after baptism as proof of serious conversion, and trust in the merciful God who willingly forgives the repentant sinner—in a healthy and dynamic balance. When the persecution of Christians ceased after 313 with the peace of Constantine, a general regulation regarding the practice of penance was established in which a tendency toward increasing rigorism is evident.

Canonical Penance

The number of Christians increased considerably from the fourth to the sixth century. Ecclesial life became better organized. The regime of canonical penance was established as the ecclesial regulation for the reconciliation of sinners, a move later crystallized in the sacrament of penance.

Instructions *(canones)* were promulgated in this period by local synods and councils with a view toward a uniform regulation for the penance required for Christians who fall back into serious sin after baptism. Augustine distinguished among three forms of penance in one of his sermons (*Sermo* 52): (1) the penance that the catechumen does as an expression of repentance in relation to his or her earlier existence in order to receive a new life through baptism, so that all sins are forgiven; (2) the daily experience of contrition that extends over daily sins; (3) a form of penance imposed by the church as an obligation for very serious sins deliberately committed after baptism. Augustine calls these sins "deadly wounds" from which the Christian can be saved only by means of a powerful medicine offered by the church in canonical penance.

Ecclesial canonical penance occurred in three phases: the repentant sinner made him- or herself known to the bishop (*publicatio sui*), who then formally designated the person a penitent. This happened in a liturgical gathering on Ash Wednesday or on a Sunday in the presence of the community. The rite of entrance into the Order of Penitents was thus public (the penitent was strewn with ash and wore a rough penitential garment), but the confession took place only before the bishop, who had to ensure that concealed sins were not made known. The term *public penance*, which is sometimes used for this period, refers only to the visibility of the penitent as such, not to a public confession of sins.

The second phase consisted in the "sojourn" in which these sinners were held to a strict way of life, which included fasting and mortification, with scourging, withholding of sexual relations, and the obligation to perform works of mercy and charity. The bishop determined the duration and the weight of the obligations.

When the bishop judged that the penitent had satisfied the necessary obligations *(satisfactio)*, a third phase followed that was again expressed liturgically in the presence of the community. The penitent was reconciled *(reconciliatio)* by means of the laying on of hands and the kiss of peace. Afterwards, the reconciled penitent was readmitted to full participation in the Eucharist.

Recent historical research has pointed out that being assigned to the Order of Penitents was not to be regarded as excommunication. The penitents belonged to the church as an "order" *(ordo poenitentium)*, just as the catechumens formed an order, and the hierarchy, too, was divided into orders. The penitents were temporarily not admitted to communion, but they remained members of the church who had to go through a penitential process. The other members, the "saints" of the church, were invited to pray for their conversion and to support them in their life of penitence. In this penitential system, which clearly exhibits rigoristic features, the idea grew of an "official" intercession for the forgiveness of sins via the ecclesial community. Seen from a historical perspective, we can say that the first "confessor," as it were, was Mother Church. It is here that we begin to see a sacramental character, although it was not yet regarded as a sacrament.

The Crisis of Rigorism

The regime of canonical penance faced a crisis. The practice fell into disuse because of the heavy requirements of penance and a number of interdicts that also remained in force after reconciliation. Canonical penance occurred only once and, like baptism, was unrepeatable. Not surprisingly, bishops, moved by pastoral concerns, advised young people not to request this form of ecclesial intercession because the danger of sinning again was too great. Canonical penance could be imposed on married people only if both spouses agreed to it, because the interdicts required complete abstinence from marital relations for the rest of one's life. In addition, the husband was prohibited from practicing any profession or conducting business publicly. Clerics and monks were prohibited from requesting any canonical penance because they, more than others, were held to the standards of a holy life by their entrance into their *ordo*. Consequently, the request to enter into penance was postponed until the end of one's life. Bishop Caesarius of Arles (503–543) advised his faithful to make use of reconciliation at the last possible moment, at the very hour of death *in extremis*, in order to emphasize more emphatically that the requirements of penitence during one's entire life are the preparation for the final reconciliation. He did not regard final reconciliation as automatic, but rather as the crowning of a long life of penance. Thus, canonical penance fell into crisis and became dysfunctional.[3]

The question remains as to whether the Christian who was aware of having committed a serious sin was permitted to participate in holy communion. In order to prevent the Eucharist from being received by the unworthy, notorious sinners were asked to withhold themselves from participation in communion. The great majority of sinners had to abstain temporarily and, with prayer and conversion, reconcile themselves with God and other believers. The penance lasted until the memory of their sins no longer disturbed them inwardly because their penance gradually freed them from their attachment to sin. When they judged themselves to be living once again in friendship with God, they were permitted to receive the Eucharist, which removed the rest of their sin. That is the solution that was used during this period of crisis. The rest of the faithful did not receive communion frequently during this period, given their anxiety over God's judgment and respect for the sacredness of the Eucharist. As a result, bishops had to impose minimal requirements and invite their Christians to receive communion at least on the most important holy days—Christmas, Easter, and Pentecost.

In conclusion, let us review the process of development: a stronger rigorism led to a practical abandonment of canonical penance. In actual practice, such penance was reserved for a small minority of Christians and still existed in abbreviated form as an immediate preparation for death. A situation of necessity developed at the pastoral level: the experience of penitence suffered from a sacramental vacuum. Penance took on its own form of experience in monastic life. Here is where the underground railway of confession of sins came into play as an expedient to spiritual direction and as the exercise of humility that would later be acknowledged as the sacramental rite of the forgiveness of sins.

Tariff Penance

The transition to the second period took a certain amount of time. In 589, with the synod of Toledo, the bishops of Spain reacted against a practice of penance that employed frequent forgiveness of sins. This divergence from canonical penance was resolutely rejected as detestable and presumptuous. The same practice was unanimously approved at the synod of Chalon-sur-Saône in 653: "Sinners may present themselves several times to a confessor who hears their confession and imposes an appropriate penance." This form accommodated the needs of those sinful believers who were deterred from canonical penance. At the end of the sixth century and during the seventh, the form of penance that was current in Anglo-Saxon/Irish and Celtic monastic life spread to the continent through the missionary activity of Columbanus and his disciples Boniface and Willebrord.

No communal liturgical celebration took place; no penitential garment was worn; nor did the penitent occupy a separate place at a distance from the church. This simple rite of penance consisted in a private confession to a priest who pronounced absolution (still in the form of a supplication to God), imposed an appropriate penance according to his judgment, and granted permission for participation in holy communion, just as in the Eastern churches.

A conflict with canonical penance arose with the introduction of this form, which was also called "insular" penance (from *insula*, island), while the former was known as the "Mediterranean Sea" form in geographical distinction from the Irish pattern. The Irish form was promulgated by the Fourth Lateran Council in 1215, and later by the fourteenth session of the Council of Trent in 1551, as the official form of the sacrament of penance. The codification of penance was typical, and its repeatability and private nature were now formalized. The *Libri poenitentiales* were drawn up to assist confessors: long catalogs containing summaries of all kinds of sin with a very advanced system of nuancing. A clear penance was imposed upon each sin, usually expressed in a number of days of fasting and/or prayers, and sometimes also in almsgiving, scourging, pilgrimage, and, in the worst cases, excommunication.

This more liberal system found quick acceptance among the faithful: canonical penance was replaced by the tariff form of penance. The confessor was no longer the bishop or Mother Church, but rather the cleric with the penitential book. The two forms coexisted briefly during the Carolingian reformation: canonical penance was required for serious public sins while the private form sufficed for the rest. The private form became the normal practice and is best characterized as *tariff penance*. Here the emphasis was on the detailed confession of sins, with the number and circumstances, which provided the occasion for an exact assessment of the tariff of the works of penance.

In some ways, tariff penance resembled a juridical procedure in which a well-defined penance was imposed in proportion to the extent of the transgression of the commandments and ecclesial interdictions. This usage was linked to the German custom of *Wehrgeld* in which the restoration of an offense could be "paid," the guilt bought off and compensated by means of a proportionate sum of money. Indeed, this was a generous ruling as a means of avoiding the vengeful nature of the form of reparation represented by "an eye for an eye, a tooth for a tooth." However, the root of later financial abuses was already present when features from civil judgment and justice were adopted for the process of exoneration from sin.

Sadly, the abuses were not long in coming. It was possible to replace the imposed penance *(commutatio):* for example, the number of fast days could be converted into alms or prayers. At first this remained limited to emergencies, as in the case of a sick or elderly person who could not fast and was thus allowed to exchange the penance for prayers. Things deteriorated when it became possible to buy off the penance *(redemptio):* a sum of money was given to someone who would carry out the penance as a surrogate *(substitutio).*

Originally, this was probably well intentioned; however, the authenticity of the conversion was open to doubt if a person permitted the penance to be carried out by others, such as serfs or priests. Priests were allowed to pray and offer Masses for the remission of sins. In the monasteries monks were ordained to the priesthood in order to offer such Masses for the forgiveness of the sins of both the living and the deceased. Tables of equivalence were established—for example, one year of fasting could be exchanged for thirty Masses offered by a priest for twenty pieces of gold. Penance was clearly reduced to a formal practice in this system. At the end of this regime, the confession itself came to the foreground as penance because of the humiliation and shame that accompanied it. We find evidence in courtly literature that sins were even confessed to the horse or the sword—if no priest was available—because confession of sins is regarded, in and of itself, as a form of penance.

From a hermeneutic perspective, we may interpret this evolution as an aberration. It overly accentuates the detailed confession of sins. This practice was maintained in the following centuries, and the process of reconciliation was pressed into a juridical context: a judgment of the degree of sinfulness.

The reversal of the sequence of actions in the process of reconciliation was another important difference from the previous period. Absolution was now given before the penance was completed. Louis-Marie Chauvet characterized this alteration not only as an evolution but also as an audacious revolution and a "substantial turning upside down."[4] This process would also fall into crisis.

The Twelfth Century

The twelfth century marked the beginning of a third period in the development of penance, although its liturgical form did not change. Spirituality mounted a healthy reaction against the empty tariff system by emphasizing the interior experience of conversion. Theologically, scholasticism brought about a systematization of the seven sacraments, in which the regime of penance was accepted and acknowledged as a sacrament.

Peter Abelard (1079–1142) is a trustworthy witness of the shift in experience, and he provided the impetus to a new theological reflection on the meaning of reconciliation with God. The Dominican scholar Marie-Dominique Chenu characterized Abelard as the first "modern" person, who caused a subversive shock in his time by giving priority in morality to subjective intention over the objectivism of natural law. His point of departure lies in his vision of what sin is.

Abelard regarded sin as an interior consent to evil, a contempt of God *(contemptus Dei)*. The proper cause of the forgiveness of sins could not be situated in a formal practice, but rather in the interior state of contrition, a remorse that proceeds from true love of God. This authentic repentance *(contritio)* removes the sin immediately. But why do confession and penance remain necessary? Abelard regarded the necessity and value of confession as willed by God as the outward means of forgiveness. Indeed, one of the components of true contrition was that the penitent was determined to receive the sacrament, if possible. The priest's absolution was more a prayer of intercession in favor of the penitent than an indicative pronouncement.

Abelard's position on the pardoning *contritio* was repeated in two other sources dating from the middle of the twelfth century: the *Decretum Gratiani*, the source of all later canonical collections, and the *Sentences (Libri Sententiarum)* of Peter Lombard, the source for the later scholastic tractates.

The prevailing concept of "sacrament" was applied systematically in theological reflection to the existing practice of penance. Following Augustine, the sacrament was defined as the visible sign of God's invisible grace. The sign *(signum)* stands in relation to the cause *(causa)*. Grace is the end result *(res tantum)* of the celebration of the sacrament that is simply called the sign *(sacramentum tantum)* in the liturgical context. In order to avoid creating the impression that the sign automatically causes grace, scholastic thought provided an intermediate category, *res et sacramentum*, as the first effect of the pure sign that is the cause of the final pardon. This intermediate effect created space for one's personal agreement in faith. Applying this to the sacrament of penance, we see the following structure: the visible actions of the penitent are regarded as a pure sign *(poenitentia exterior)*, the interior condition of contrition is a *res et sacramentum*, that is, the sign and cause of the remission of sins *(res tantum)*.

While the facet of absolution was overlooked in early scholasticism, it returned to the foreground when the Aristotelian "form–matter" schema, the basic structure of every substance, was applied to penance in high scholasticism. The confession and the penance of the sinner were regarded as matter, while the priest's words of absolution were the *forma*. Over time, absolution would assume an important place in the sacrament of penance as its constitutive element. William of Auvergne (died in 1249) points to the necessity of an initial disposition *(dispositio)* in the penitent, who had to exhibit at least partial contrition *(attritio)*, which occurs, in fact, when the individual presents him- or herself for confession. This *attritio* is elevated to perfect contrition, the foundation for God's forgiveness, through the invocation of God's forgiveness in the priest's absolution. Up to this point the formula was still intercessory: "May God forgive you...." An appeal was made to the priest in order to ascertain that the penitent attained this high degree of contrition. On the basis of this insight, the sacrament of penance assumed an integral place in the ongoing conversion of the penitent, situated between partial and perfect contrition.

The Contribution of Thomas Aquinas

The unique contribution of Thomas Aquinas (1225–1274) lies in the clear confirmation of the efficacy of the confession. Thomas made the remission of sins the final result of the sacrament of penance as one undivided reality in which four elements exist in a mutual, constitutive bond. He understood the penitent's acts of contrition, confession, and penance as *quasi materia*, while the priest's absolution constitutes the *forma* that is now formulated in the indicative—"I absolve you" *(ego te absolvo)*—as also used in baptism and confirmation.

Thomas refers to the power of the keys that is entrusted to priests. Absolution is the instrumental cause of God's remission of sins. Duns Scotus's theology did not follow Thomas's unified vision; Scotus represented the priest's absolution as the easy way willed by God to obtain the remission of sins through the sacrament of penance. He regarded the way of justification without the sacrament by means of personal conversion as the difficult path in which we trust in God's free will to remit sins if sufficient contrition is expressed. But we are never certain of this.

Protestant and Catholic Reforms

From a hermeneutic perspective, this last formulation was unfortunate insofar as it unduly emphasized the role of absolution. It may well have been the easy way, but did it do justice to penitents' authentic experiences? The sacrament threatened to become an automatic means that, on the basis of priestly power, forgives sins irrespective of one's state of contrition. In fact, this happened during the period of nominalism in which Luther grew up and against which his sharp reaction is to be understood.

Calvin would make a juridical distinction between the required discipline of confession as a form of ecclesial administration of justice and the consolation confession that a believer with a heavy conscience can always confide to the pastor. The Council of Trent reacted to the Reformers' denial of the sacramental character of confession and strongly emphasized the unique efficacy of the sacrament.

The Catholic Reformation witnessed a double tendency. On the one hand, casuistry accentuated the correct determination of serious sins and the free disposition of the sinner. Therefore, the confessor had to possess the necessary knowledge of moral theology and ecclesiastical law. On the other hand, there was a tendency toward spiritual direction by means of a devotional confession to which all believers were invited, even if they had committed no mortal sin. At the same time, Christians who had grown holy on their journey could continue their formation.

Frequent Confession

The frequency of confession increased greatly in the nineteenth and twentieth centuries. The preaching of religious, missionaries, and eucharistic movements stimulated and encouraged this practice. Regular confession was regarded as self-evident in a good Christian life. The confessor was a marriage counselor, psychologist, psychiatrist, and shepherd, knowledgeable in the law and expert in morality.

A Third Crisis

Frequent confession remained the practice until this climax in the practice of confession was broken fairly suddenly in the middle of the twentieth century by changing sociocultural contexts. Secularization, an obscuring of the awareness of God, opposition to institutions and ideologies, developments in the relationship between priest and faithful within the church, neo-individualism, the demand for personal autonomy, and the subjective self-sufficiency of the modern individual—all these shook the foundations of confessional practice and understanding. Reconciliation fell into a deep crisis for the third time.

Vatican II: Renewal and Revision of Reconciliation

Vatican II and the bishops' synod of 1983 sought to respond to the crisis in the practice of private confession. The communal dimension of the sacrament came to attention once again, offering the possibility for a communal celebration of Christian reconciliation.[5] These communal celebrations, in which absolution is given without previous individual confession, are subject to certain conditions. The church wants to guard against communal celebrations being regarded as the "normal" form of this sacrament. Still, the history of the sacrament offers good reasons to claim that we are entering a *fourth period*, in which the two forms, private confession and communal services, will be made available as *complete* forms of the sacrament of reconciliation.

The Fourth Period: Reconciliation in the Postmodern Era

Because of the profound crisis in private confession, a rethinking of reconciliation in postmodern terms is urgently needed. But it does not need to be implemented too quickly. Care needs to be taken to provide necessary catechesis and guidance with regard to the awareness of sin and the earnest conversion of heart. From a pastoral perspective, communal celebrations could become too "cheap." They could become choked again in formalism. The transition from the first to the second period of reconciliation took place over several generations. What is really important and crucial right now is that the faithful are guided on their path of conversion to reconciliation.

Attitudes of Openness and Conversion

We have learned from history that rigorism cannot be a good teacher; thus a reintroduction of an Order of Penitents is not an option, nor is strict penance in which sinners are kept at a distance. On the contrary, the ecclesial community must be an inviting community in which sinners are welcome ("a welcoming community"), where they are supported on their journey of conversion by the prayers of others, and where they are able to recognize the outstretched hand of a merciful God in the open hands of their fellow believers.[6]

We have also learned from the transition from the second to the third period that formalism can be conquered only by an inwardly profound and evangelical spirituality. The believer can recognize completely the seriousness of sin, appreciate the negative consequences of bad behavior, be converted from an egotistical way of life, and experience the beneficial gift of reconciliation only by following the path of interiority. It is of fundamental importance that the faithful develop the virtues of repentance and contrition *(contritio)* and practice them in their daily lives. That is where the fundamental and sure ground for reconciliation is found across all of history as the consistent and crucial pattern. The configuration of this sacrament for our time and the future must put the element of conversion and contrition at the center. The sacrament is a gift of God, who comes to meet the believer in Christ and the Holy Spirit. The central text for absolution in the new ritual of reconciliation expresses this quite beautifully:

> God, the Father of mercies,
> through the death and resurrection of his Son
> has reconciled the world to himself
> and sent the Holy Spirit among us

for the forgiveness of sins;
through the ministry of the church
may God grant you pardon and peace,
and I absolve you of your sins
in the name of the Father, and of the Son, and of the
    Holy Spirit.

This promise of reconciliation in the power of the Holy Spirit is also offered in communal celebrations. Without unduly emphasizing one element at the expense of the other, we can gradually discover the degree to which the other elements of confession and penance still belong to the heart of the sacrament. The church must discover, out of pastoral solicitude, how best to express its "instrumentality." This is a modest offer, but whoever accepts it may experience actual forgiveness in the name of God through the sacrament.

The church is capable of adapting the form of the liturgy so that it can determine when absolution, individual or collective, can be given. Keeping in mind the historical legacy and the current *sensus fidelium*, a dual approach is called for: the private celebration of the sacrament of reconciliation remains a benefit for those faithful who confide to a priest their personal path of conversion, so that the pardon is personally and meaningfully promised. By this means life receives a silent glimmer after a process of inner conversion.

In the communal celebration the ecclesial dimension and the solidarity in sin and reconciliation take on a stronger, more visible form than in the private celebration. The resistance on the part of many believers with regard to private confession, for whatever reason, is an inescapable factor that the hierarchy must take into account so as not to set needless conditions for admission to the communal celebrations.[7] Of course, these communal celebrations must meet a number of liturgical requirements. In this respect, the introduction of a yearly day of penance (such as the Jewish Day of Atonement) is not a good option. It is better to provide a communal celebration at regular times—for example, in the week before Christmas, Easter, Pentecost, and All Saints—so that the faithful have the opportunity to participate consciously several times a year. In so doing, the sequence of penance followed by absolution could be restored as well, so that the celebration is experienced as the completion of a path of conversion and penance that the believer has already fulfilled in his or her daily life. The sacrament is the rendering and crowning of conversion and reconciliation with one another, now sealed by God, promised in the name of the risen Lord and received as a gift of the Holy Spirit. The sacrament is a celebration in thankfulness for God's free gift of forgiveness and reconciliation.

A Place for the Community in Reconciliation

Although it remains true that an authentic inner conversion of heart *(contritio)* is viewed theologically as the sufficient foundation for God's forgiveness, the call upon ecclesial intercession is still not superfluous. The ecclesial community is invited to play a role in the faithful's path of conversion. It can help them to arrive at reconciliation with God and one another. The sacrament elevates a partial contrition to a perfect contrition, which is no longer thought of as the scholastic intermediate effect *(res et sacramentum)* as expressed in metaphysical terms, but is rather regarded as the concrete ecclesial peace *(pax cum ecclesia)* that grants admission to the peace of God *(pax cum Deo)*. It is to Karl Rahner's credit that he valued this insight from the patristic church and so replaced the scholastic, abstract concept with the visible relation to the community of faith.[8] It is important to retain this vision for the future of the sacrament, namely, that reconciliation is an actual sign of atonement with God with and within the ecclesial community. In this manner, the church fulfills its mission as a foundational sacrament in service to the coming of the kingdom of God (the eschatological dimension), in service to people in their search for liberation from guilt and need for forgiveness. When a vacuum has developed through the crisis in the practice of private confession, "a servant church" cannot allow the faithful to wait too long for an accommodation that they can experience as a sign, a gift of God's mercy.

The Spirit's Gift of Peace

This is the most profound meaning of the gift of the Spirit in this sacrament, the Spirit that cleanses and renews (as the Pentecost Sequence *Veni Sancte Spiritus* puts it) and recreates that which was barren and dead. The fruit of reconciliation is a new life in peace with God and with one another. The true meaning *(réfiguration)* of this sacrament is that God grants forgiveness to the sinner who exhibits contrition and a change of heart. This faith conviction grew in ancient Israel: God allowed himself to be known as the Creator and the God of salvation, justice, and mercy in Israel's experience of faith. Jesus is the ultimate revelation of this God, who died for our sins, the Lamb of God who takes away the sins of the world. Since the twelfth century, Western theology has attempted to comprehend this given of faith by placing it in metaphysical categories. A postmodern approach points out the limitations of the ontological vision of God: this is the god of our thoughts and projections, not the true God who allows himself to be known from the evidence of Scripture.

We have seen how Jean-Luc Marion's philosophy distances itself from the god of metaphysical thought *(idole conceptuelle)*. Marion recommends that theologians turn back to the biblical, evangelical message of God's self-revelation in Jesus as the icon of the invisible (Col 1:15), as pure gift *(don)*, to the abandonment *(abandon)* of his Son, for the forgiveness *(pardon)* of evil. When the sacrament of reconciliation is viewed in this context, it becomes clear that the image of God that functioned most strongly in this sacrament was the spectator God who judges, the all-seeing eye that frightens people and makes them anxious. This is really just a representation of God; it is not the God who revealed himself in Jesus and who grants forgiveness as a free gift *(don)* to every sinner who has a change of heart.[9]

In his subtle analysis of the eye and the triangle—"God sees me. No one curses here" —Dutch philosopher Cornelis Verhoeven is close to Jean-Luc Marion's postmodern interpretation. He posits that the "religious" category is used to give a definite character to our own words and thoughts. That is a human projection in the direction of the divine. In the attitude of faith, however, the direction of the gaze is reversed: it is directed from God to us. "And by this we will know that we are from the truth and will reassure our hearts before him whenever our hearts condemn us: for God is greater than our hearts, and he knows everything" (1 John 3:19–20). "It is almost incidental, like a poetic slip in what is further a fairly moralizing context, but it seems to me to be of essential importance.

The opposition between inside and outside, one's own interiority and the opinion of others, is overtaken by a comprehensive gaze that extends further than the anxiety of our own heart with its secret, misleading and mistrustful thoughts."[10]

The Sacrament of the Anointing of the Sick

Suffering and death are the greatest challenges to have confronted humans in every age. No one is exempt from the experience of vulnerability and physical mortality. All the various religious traditions search for a response to these challenges.

The Christian response to suffering and death is rooted in the mystery of the death and resurrection of the Son of God, Jesus Christ. He shared the human condition with us, even unto death itself. But in his dying, he won a victory over death. We celebrate this central mystery of our faith in the Eucharist. The anointing of the sick also celebrates this mystery and its victory.

Historical Overview of Anointing

Anointing of the sick developed in the course of history in imitation of Jesus' actions with regard to sick and suffering people and as a celebration of his death and resurrection. These experiences of a "broken existence," with their anthropological context, are thus taken up in the Christian celebration of the sacraments. Additionally, the celebration of the anointing of the sick also functions as a life ritual, a rite of passage where one passes from a former situation to a new status. Of course, anointing of the sick is more than just a rite of passage. It is the proclamation of faith in Jesus' death and resurrection with regard to the suffering person, with a renewed gift of the Holy Spirit as consolation and (spiritual) strengthening.[11]

New Testament Witness

In solidarity with Jesus' acts on behalf of sick individuals, the Twelve received a particular solicitude for the sick in their commission. "They cast out many demons, and anointed with oil many who were sick and cured them" (Mark 6:13). In the Letter of James we see how concretely members of the young Christian community associate with sick fellow believers: "Are any among you sick? They should call for the elders of the church and have them pray over them, anointing them with oil in the name of the Lord. The prayer of faith will save the sick, and the Lord will raise them up; and anyone who has committed sins will be forgiven" (Jas 5:14–15).

The Patristic Age

In the postapostolic and patristic periods the custom of anointing the sick in a context of faithful prayer by those most responsible in the Christian community developed into "a holy sign, something in the genre of a sacrament" (*pertinet ad genus sacramenti* [Letter from Pope Innocent I to Bishop Decentius of Gubbio in 416]). This anointing of the sick bore the characteristics of an ecclesial faith interpretation of Jesus' resurrection.

Christians in the first centuries attached great importance to the oil that was consecrated by the bishop for anointing the sick. This consecrated oil was given to the priests and the faithful so that they could anoint the sick with it. Anointing of the sick belonged to the most important expressions of pastoral care in the ecclesial community: a holy sign, somewhat comparable to the great sacred signs such as baptism and Eucharist. This period was not yet cognizant of a strictly delineated concept of "sacrament" that only later was defined as being applicable to the "seven sacraments" beginning in 1140 with Peter Lombard. It would be anachronistic to make a direct equation of such anointings with what we understand today to constitute the sacraments. They are expressions of faith in a framework of prayers, whereby the salvific effect of the anointing concerns both the physical and the spiritual well-being of the sick. That a great deal of value was attached to this holy sign is evident from the prohibition against giving this anointing to penitents, that is, those faithful who were doing formal penance for serious sins and who were also prevented from participating in holy communion (from the same letter of Innocent I).

In being linked with the penitential system, the anointing of the sick was postponed until after the reconciliation of the penitents, which gradually occurred increasingly at the end of life. In this way the anointing of the sick, together with the ecclesial regulations concerning canonical penance, shifted to the deathbed. In the meantime, Bishop Caesarius of Arles (503–543) recommended to his priests that the anointing may be calmly given to all sick people so that they may be strengthened in their faith and place their trust in God. Pastoral solicitude plays a role in such recommendations: Caesarius reacted against all forms of superstition and wished to keep his faithful away from the magical healing practices of the pagan Germans. The effect of the anointing of the sick came to be regarded increasingly on a spiritual level: strengthening of faith and forgiveness of sins, since sin was regarded as one of the sources of the illness.

Carolingian Age

A more uniform ecclesial regulation concerning the administration of the anointing was formulated during the Carolingian period. The sacramental minister was now exclusively the priest. Less importance was attached to the consecration of the oil by the bishop, and priests were also allowed to consecrate the oil themselves. The anointing became part of the penance that was completed upon the deathbed. In practice the anointing of the sick evolved into "extreme unction" *(extrema unctio)*, as a supplement to the remission of sins. We could say that before the eighth century it was an exception for the anointing of the sick to be followed by death, while after the eleventh century this became the normal state of affairs—the anointing *in extremis*, extreme unction as an immediate preparation for death, an ultimate and complete cleansing from sin and the remnants of sin, so that the soul's transition to eternal salvation can take place without any problems. The effects of the anointing occurred exclusively at the spiritual level.

Scholasticism

When scholastic theology developed a systematic doctrine of the seven sacraments with a precisely delineated concept of ecclesial sacraments, this "fifth" sacrament took place in the context of anointing on one's deathbed in conjunction with the forgiveness of sins and followed by the final communion or *viaticum*. Extreme unction preserved the bond with the sacrament of penance in this system of sacraments, with the priest as the exclusive minister. Only the dying could receive this sacrament.

Theologically, the specific effects of extreme unction could only be situated on a spiritual level. Thomas Aquinas, who attached importance to the symbolic character of every sacrament, is a good example. Thomas starts his reflection with the act of anointing and sees therein a medicinal symbol: via the anointing of the body—all of the senses in Aquinas's time—a "spiritual anointing" takes place, an anointing of the soul, in order to heal the soul of all weakness (*infirmitas*, lack of strength) caused by sin. In fact, sins were forgiven by the sacrament of penance, and anointing completed the forgiveness by removing from the soul all remnants of sin (*reliquiae peccati*, as Aquinas's teacher Albert the Great had already held). The unhealthy, weakened condition of the soul was healed so that it was completely ready to approach eternal life. That result (*res tantum* in scholastic terminology) was brought about in the dying person by the sacrament (*sacramentum tantum*).

Thomas Aquinas connects this grace of anointing to the faith of the person and the faith of the church. The effect is caused not automatically but rather by means of an intermediate effect (*res et sacramentum*) of an inner surrender in faith of the person who entrusts him- or herself to God. This inner *devotio* consists of an absolute orientation to God, the will to open oneself completely to God in faith, hope, and love. The dying individual receives the grace of spiritual healing on the basis of this faithful surrender, as well as the perfection that admits him or her to eternal bliss. It was this Thomistic theology that helped to bring about the restriction of the anointing to the dying.[12]

Anointing and the Catholic Reformation

The Protestant Reformers sought to make anointing available to those not in danger of death. They wanted to return to the practice common in the first few centuries as an anointing of everyone who was sick, including those who were not threatened by death.

In reaction to the vision of the Reformers, the Council of Trent in 1551 adopted the Thomistic view of anointing as well as its form of celebration as practiced since the eleventh century. The concluding texts avoided limiting the sacrament to the dying, and they also asserted, among other things, that physical health was sometimes recovered if it was salutary for the person. While not excluding physical healing, they did subordinate it to the salvation of the soul.

The council fathers sought to oppose the Reformation's proposition that the text of James intended a special charism of healing, a special gift that was only given to the apostles in the beginning of the church. Instead the Council of Trent asserted that anointing the sick is a true and unique sacrament, instituted by Christ, made known by James, and now entrusted to the church in order to give consolation and relief to all the sick via its administration by priests.

Twentieth-Century Renewal and Reform

A renewal in the current practice of extreme unction occurred in the middle of the twentieth century. The historical studies of Antoine Chavasse and Bernard Botte on the anointing of the sick in the first centuries, along with the liturgical movement, helped bring about a critical review of the then-current practice and theology. These scholars concluded that this sacrament ought to be removed from the context of death to become once again a sacrament for the sick, as was originally intended in the text of James and the most ancient liturgical practice.

In the middle of the century the congregation of the Roman rite approved new rituals that reflected the new perspective. After many centuries this sacrament became once again a ritual, a prayer, and a sacrament for the sick and not only for the dying. This movement was confirmed by the Second Vatican Council, and in the *Constitution on the Sacred Liturgy* (*Sacrosanctum Concilium*) we see a first deposition on this:

> "Extreme Unction," which may also and more fittingly be called "anointing of the sick," is not a sacrament for those only who are at the point of death. Hence, as soon as any one of the faithful begins to be in danger of death

from sickness or old age, the appropriate time for him to receive this sacrament has certainly already arrived. (no. 73, December 4, 1963)

The theological contents and the efficacy of this sacrament are described with greater precision in the *Dogmatic Constitution on the Church* (*Lumen Gentium*) issued the following year:

By the sacred anointing of the sick and the prayer of her priests, the whole Church commends those who are ill to the suffering and glorified Lord, asking that He may lighten their sufferings and save them. She exhorts them, moreover, to contribute to the welfare of the whole People of God by uniting themselves freely with the passion and death of Christ. (no. 11, November 21, 1964)

This is clearly no longer the sacrament of one's final moments: the sick who experience the sacrament receive the status of "anointed" in the ecclesial community and there give the evidence of their union with the suffering Christ in surrender to God's will. For this reason, the new ritual also provides communal celebrations in which a greater number of elderly and sick persons can receive this sacrament, alongside individual anointing. This also occurs with pilgrimages and days set aside for the infirm, parish-based Sunday rites for the ill, and celebrations in hospitals and nursing homes, without the anxiety of imminent death.

The anthropological context for anointing has been shifted to the situation of the seriously ill or elderly faithful. The sick person becomes a sign of surrender in the context of the church's prayer. In this way, he or she still has a mission within the church and still contributes to the well-being of the entire people. The sacramental act has a particular significance as the conferral of meaning upon illness and mortality in the light of faith. It is here that the eschatological dimension can be stressed, the definitive character of this witness in the face of death. The sick person has his or her ultimate destination in view and anticipates it in a certain sense via a surrender in faith. This is a clarification that does not remove the crisis of serious illness or old age. This sacrament stands as a sign of healing and witness to union with Christ in suffering and resurrection before the final destination, the eschatological judgment that is anticipated in time.

Anointing and the Holy Spirit

In the current context, the gift of the Spirit that occurs with this sacrament is in the foreground at the same time. The central text for the anointing in the renewed ritual expresses the gift of the Holy Spirit in a most touching manner:

> Through this holy anointing
> may the Lord in his love and mercy help you
> with the grace of the Holy Spirit.
> May the Lord who frees you from sin
> save you and raise you up.

The anointing is followed by this subsequent prayer:

> Lord Jesus Christ, our Redeemer,
> by the grace of your Holy Spirit
> cure the weakness of your servant N. . . .

In a postmodern age, the attention given to this sacrament can clearly be directed to the communal dimension and the gift of the Spirit, as a silent glimmer of participation in the divine mystery of self-offering, resembling Jesus, the icon of the invisible. Whereas Thomistic theology moved in the abstract terms of the causality of grace, theological reflection can now proceed from the language of the self-giving God in Christ and in the unselfishly gratuitous gift of the Holy Spirit as the effect of this sacrament.

The Holy Spirit is given anew in this situation, which is pregnant with the experience of finitude. The Spirit's comfort and consolation are a source of strength to the infirm believer. The field of experience of this sacrament has been expanded to the situation of the sick, who consciously solemnize a pious action. They become themselves the icon of the suffering Christ, identified with the human Jesus who passed through death.

The identification with Christ takes place from another perspective as well. The faithful who care for the sick and accompany them with their prayer are also identified with Christ. They profess his love to the infirm. They give hands to Christ through their own caring hands. Through their eyes, Christ regards the ill with compassion and mercy. This happens in the renewed gift of the Spirit, who consoles and relieves, with a silent glimmer of God's inaccessible light.

In a renewed sacramental theology, then, the accent no longer falls on the almost automatic result of cause and effect in a sign that, as it were, causes the effect of grace of its own accord. The sacrament is experienced as a symbolic action whereby this life situation is placed in the light of faith before God and whereby we know ourselves to be carried by God's nearness, becoming new people in the gift of the Spirit. So the anointing of the sick, like every other sacrament, is a symbolic expression in language and sign of an attitude of faith that transposes reality against the horizon of the most profound meaning. In this way, the sacraments function as metaphors of our existence in the symbolic order.

Healing and Anointing

The sacrament of anointing is neither a magical healing of the sick nor competition with medical science. The healing that we have in mind here lies on another plane, one that regards the individual most profoundly. It transposes reality to a level of experience in which the individual's relationship to God is expressed and lived out. Rather than being a flight from reality, however, this is reality at its highest or most profound level: the ultimate destination. That which "actually" happens takes place here in the proclamation of faith and in the anointing, which is indeed a real anointing of the body as a symbol of healing in union with the suffering and resurrected Lord. In this way Christians experience this sacrament as a beneficial sign. If the person experiences positive physical effects as well, as a result of the acceptance and the strength that flow forth from this sacrament on the spiritual level, this is "beneficial for the entire person." We place a faithful sign as the rendering of our trust in God in this sacrament, and from this point the infirm individual can integrate the painful situation into his or her life in a new, more profound manner. This new level of existence is not something that the sick person has to forge alone; rather, it is done with the support of fellow believers.

Minister(s) of Anointing

Given the new role of this sacrament in the care of the sick, the question has arisen whether someone other than the priest can act as the minister. The arguments cited in favor of this include the shortage of priests, the presence of nurses and chaplains from the sick ward who must sometimes call upon a priest from outside, the possibility of "extraordinary ministers" such as we already have for holy communion, and the availability of deacons. The ecclesial regulation can be adapted for this in the future.

Presently, the priest is called the "proper" *(proprius)* minister of this sacrament, but we can still consider the possibility of appointing others, especially if the sacrament is set free from its close connection with the sacrament of reconciliation, of which the priest is the exclusive minister. We appeal too easily to the practice of the early church, where the faithful took the oil home with them to anoint their sick. Indeed, during this phase the anointing of the sick belonged to the "holy signs" that occurred in the church, but there was as yet no systematic doctrine about the seven sacraments. Twelfth-century thinkers did not regard every form of anointing of the sick as a sacrament. At that time it was a question of the final anointing at the end of life. Because of this, the ecclesiastical regulation continues to state that the priest is the regular, proper minister of this sacrament.

Practically speaking, this does not prevent other fellow believers from performing the laying on of hands, praying, and anointing the seriously ill. These are very meaningful occurrences, but they have not yet attained the rank of the "official" sacrament. This sacrament has the potential for a development in the collaboration between the lay faithful and ordained ministers. It is normal for the ordained office to be represented in order to acknowledge the anointing as a sacrament. In line with the interpretation of "presbyters" in the text of James, we can consider placing permanent deacons in this category: they share in the official solicitude for the entire community. At the time the Letter of James was written, the ecclesial organization of the priestly office was not yet so structured that we can assert that only those whom we currently call priests fall into that category. By extension, we can consider the officially appointed chaplains in the care of the sick, who carry out their vocation in the name of the church without being ordained. To the extent that the church mandates that they exercise this spiritual office to the infirm, we should not rule out the possibility that they, too, can be allowed to officiate in the sacramental celebration of the anointing of the sick. To the extent that, in the evolution of the self-understanding of the church community, these chaplains are clearly acknowledged as official representatives of the entire church in their care for the sick, not much more stands in the way theologically of allowing them to act as sacramental ministers.[13]

In the meantime, nothing prevents anointings with prayers and the laying on of hands from being conducted without their being regarded as a sacrament. In this context, it is worth considering Gisbert Greshake's proposal. First of all, the definition of "sacrament" as strictly understood was only formulated in the twelfth century, when people began to regard the final anointing in an eschatological perspective.[14] Greshake holds that the meaning of this "fifth" sacrament has been all too easily skewed in the direction of a simple anointing of the sick at the expense of the eschatological sense of suffering and death. By changing this sacrament to a mere anointing of the sick, we miss the church's highly urgent commission to proclaim the ultimate meaning of our life beyond death and to express our baptismal faith, especially in the hope of eternal life, in a sacramental action.

Greshake believes that we are in danger of giving in to the strong modern taboo about death and dying. Death continues to be a persistent taboo that may not be spoken of in our secularized culture; it is always pushed forward and pushed away. We do not dare to look directly at our mortality, and yet Christians have a message about that on the basis of their faith in the resurrection: the heart of Christian faith is precisely all about that. This is precisely where we have a unique opportunity to proclaim the Christian message in all its profundity, against the outlook of perplexity and the deficit of meaning with regard to death in our society and culture. "Illness can function as a magnifying glass. The awareness of one's approaching demise makes one's perception sharper and one's perspective more metaphysical."[15]

Greshake revisits the distinction between the greater and lesser sacraments: baptism and Eucharist are evidently the most important. All the others are either directed toward them or derived from them. He emphasizes the relation between the anointing of the sick and baptism. He characterizes anointing of the sick as a renewal of the baptismal promise in the face of death. In contrast to and confrontation with the modern "ignorance of death," the Christian community provides a clear witness to its faith and hope that after this life the faithful are hidden in God and receive new life through the Spirit. The believer's baptismal conviction is continued in his or her faithful experience of the sacrament to the sick. We celebrate this sacrament as baptized people of and for the sick. The eschatological dimension that is already present in baptism, in dying and rising with the Lord Jesus in the paschal mystery, becomes particularly acute in the anointing of the sick because the confrontation with life's end announces itself within the actual horizon of experience. In such circumstances God's saving nearness and the gift of the Spirit are experienced and even promised in God's name in the sacramental celebration. Here the church's consolation offered to the sick replaces and improves upon the abstract scholastic notion of intermediate effect *(res et sacramentum)*. Peace with God is realized through peace with the church.

The entire ecclesial community stands as the basic sacrament, a continuation of Jesus as the primordial sacrament. Rahner envisioned the following effect of the anointing of the sick at the level of the visible church community: Through their anointing these believers become more clearly engaged as members of the pilgrim and victorious church. They receive, as it were, a unique and new status as anointed within this church community. They experience their faith in the human pilgrimage toward death, but with trust and hope in their hearts that this journey also contains a passage that arrives at God. The anointed bear witness to this while living in our midst. We can see the mission and commission that they fulfill in relation to the rest of the faithful, their contribution "to the well-being of the people of God." Those among us who have received the anointing of the sick have become more conformed to Christ in a special way by this sacrament, anointed (in Greek: *christoi*) in Christ's death and resurrection in the hope of standing with him beyond death. They are an image for us, an icon of the suffering, dying, and risen Lord.

Chapter Nine
SACRAMENTS OF VOCATION: MARRIAGE AND HOLY ORDERS

In addition to the two sacraments of healing that absorb previous negative experiences of life with its finitude and deficiencies, two sacraments of vocation bring the seven to conclusion. Once again, they continue and crown the positive experiences of life in the ascending trajectory of the sacraments of initiation.

The context for the sacraments of vocation shifts its focus to the faithful commitment of adults, who on the basis of their baptism and confirmation shape their Christian lives further by taking on their calling. In so doing, they receive a renewed gift of the Spirit in order to experience their vocation as Christians in new circumstances in response to God's invitation. I will discuss the sacraments of marriage and holy orders in a postmodern context with the accent on the character of gratuitous gift, a renewed gift of the Holy Spirit that is experienced as an approach of the Other. This is a dialogue with the invisible God in the continuation of the mystery of Christ in which God brushes up against humans; it is a language of the self-giving God. God's voluntary gift becomes visible in the sacrament where people want to become a "gift" (*don*) to one another.

Marriage

From Blessing to Sacrament

The marriage ritual that was once a family matter has received the status of a sacrament in the Eastern and Western Christian churches.[1] Toward the end of the fourth century the custom began in the Greek church of inviting the bishop or a priest to invoke

God's blessing on the new couple. From the eighth century on it became more common for this blessing to take place in the church, and since that time it has become a law that the priest must bless all marriages of baptized Christians for a church wedding to be acknowledged by the civil authorities. The central ceremony in the liturgy of the East is the coronation of the married couple: the priest places crowns on the heads of the bride and groom.

In the West the blessing of the priest on what was viewed as a familial celebration was not considered a sacrament during the early centuries of Christendom. Ecclesiastical legislation became necessary with the integration of the Roman tradition—where the marriage came about by means of mutual consent (contract)—and that of the German peoples, where the first sexual intercourse (*matrimonium consummatum*) was the determining factor in the marriage contract. In accordance with canon law, from the eleventh century onward the bishops required that all marriages be blessed with a certain ceremony by a priest either inside or in front of the church. Mutual consent remained the central given, but the marriage was regarded as indissoluble only if it was also consummated by sexual intercourse.[2]

The seven Christian sacraments became fixed in scholastic theology. The rite of marriage is one of the seven acts in the church that are acknowledged as having been instituted by Christ in order to confer grace. It is an efficacious sign that realizes what it stands for. It is a visible sign and origin of invisible grace that comes into being through the solemnization of the ritual. "By declaring marriage a sacrament, the Church advanced the emancipation of one's personal life history from social and institutional constraint. The relation with God was realized not only by means of the stable arrangement of society or the solemn sublimity of the liturgy, but as much via one's personal, daily and bodily history."[3]

The Aristotelian philosophy of hylemorphism (*materia* and *forma*) provides the context in which traditional sacramental theology is formulated. The promise (*forma*) of mutual faithfulness, spoken in the presence of the priest and two witnesses as representatives of the church community elevates the mutual relation (*loco materiae*) to the status of a sacrament, a sanctifying sign.

Marriage in a Postmodern Theological Perspective

The current, postmodern approach to sacramental theology directs attention to the integration of the seven sacraments in a symbolic order, or, in Louis-Marie Chauvet's words, *"un réseau symbolique,"* a symbolic network that spreads across all of life with ecclesial celebrations of faith.[4] As a sacrament that sanctifies a relationship, marriage unites the parties as gifts to one another with the profundity of a divine union: their mutual consent is anchored in the promise of God's covenant with humanity.

In reflecting on the deeper meaning of this commitment, such as we find in the Letter to the Ephesians (5:21–33), the marriage relationship is compared to Christ's surrender to his church community: the union of husband and wife mirrors the unselfish love *(agapē)* of Christ, who remained faithful to his proclamation of the coming of God's kingdom in his person up to the cross. The married partners are thus called to love each other after Christ's own example and in the power of the Holy Sprit, with the same unselfish love and faithfulness that Jesus exhibited. They "sanctify" each other by this means. They complete their human love in the lap of divine love. This commitment "marks" them for life as bound to one another for all time in God's love and faithfulness.

Herwi Rikhof, a theologian from Utrecht in the Netherlands, considers whether a sacramental character is conferred on marriage in the same way as with the unrepeatable sacraments of baptism, confirmation, and priesthood:

> We can now declare that marriage is a new phase in people's lives, with two people agreeing to live with one another as its feature. The actions that are unique to this new phase have to do with this relationship. The sacrament of marriage has bearing on this relationship and on the actions that are bound up with it: by means of the sacrament the relationship and the actions attached to it are a part of the worship of God (in the broad sense) and they point to and signify the relationship of Christ and the Church. That is the unique characteristic of the sacrament of marriage. Seen in this way, their relationship allows two people to enter into a new relation to the

worship of God. In this perspective, marriage resembles baptism, confirmation, and ordination. It does not resemble penance. And so, it is self evident to confer a sacramental character upon marriage. Husband and wife are delegated together in the sacrament of marriage to the worship of God. Together, they also receive a part of Christ's priesthood.[5]

Chauvet's Vision

Louis-Marie Chauvet has developed a postmodern theology of the sacrament of marriage.[6] He assumes that the categories of Thomistic hylemorphism are hardly applicable to the sacrament of marriage. Marriage is no static given, but a dynamic reality that is realized anew every day in a context of fulfilling the promise that was spoken at the wedding ceremony.

The essentials of marriage are situated in the bond of mutual love (Chauvet calls this *instituant*). When two people also wish to confirm their mutual commitment of faithfulness to this love in a sacrament of the church, they join the institution that, in the church, has traditionally acquired its own formation on the basis of biblical and theological principles. Therein is stressed the goodness of the creation of humans as man and woman (Genesis 2–3), the mirroring in their faithfulness of God's union with humanity, and the symbolic realization in their mutual oneness of the oneness and love *(agapē)* between Christ and the church community.

Chauvet offers an account of the tension that exists between the subjective, spontaneous experience of the love of two people and the established institution of marriage. According to the church's confession of faith in varying contexts, the particular identity of Christian marriage represents a high ideal that deserves to be continuously pursued. This identity is based on the broader sacramentality that is present in all of creation. Creation has been penetrated by grace from the very beginning: God communicates himself to all created things.[7] In this way, the mutual love between husband and wife can be a particular manifestation of the love that God has shown in creation and covenant. This covenant is established through Christ in his personal surrender to the cross, empowered by God in the resurrection and glorification of the Son, and in the gift of the Holy Spirit. Therefore, Christian marriage has roots in the order of creation and in the christological mystery of salvation.

Love as Gift

The wedding ceremony makes this tie of love explicitly manifest and elevates human love to a participation in divine love. The promise of the couple anchors their commitment in the divine promise of grace. This is a gift in the name of God, a renewing gift of the Holy Spirit, to which the couple responds in gratitude by their faithful love. The aspects of continuous conversion to God and willingness to forgive are included in this gift. In their constantly renewed choice of each other, the couple is an icon of God's faithful love in union with the mystery of Christ. In their love, the love of God—Father, Son, and Holy Spirit—becomes visible and palpable. That is the characteristic of Christian marriage.[8]

Festival of Life

At the same time, Christian marriage can be characterized as a "festival of life." In the ritual landscape of contemporary society there is a decline in Sunday observance, but on the other hand there is also a flourishing of new rituals, certainly with regard to rites of passage at transitional moments of life. "A festival is based upon four pillars in a general phenomenological sense: (1) the contrast with regard to the normal daily pattern: a festival is something other; it stops the treadmill for an instant; it is a place of freedom; (2) an occasion: something or someone to be celebrated is the axis upon which the festival turns, with regard to content; (3) a ritual play: feasting is something you *do;* you play with words and deeds; (4) the solidarity group: feasting is something you do together."[9]

These four dimensions are identifiable in the marriage ceremony. A festival, certainly with marriage, is still a deeply rooted form of ritual. Even in a secular context we speak spontaneously about "our wedding ceremony" and "the most beautiful day of our lives." The festival marks a moment of "interruption" in time. It is a *kairos* occurrence—the opportune, convenient moment—that stops the continuously running *chronos*—undifferentiated time. We celebrate by temporarily distancing ourselves from daily praxis in order to express the deeper meaning of life.

The mutual promise made in marriage is situated in the community of solidarity with a superabundance of symbolic acts and a profusion of words. It is also situated in the broader overall significance of the foundational event. By bringing time to a temporary halt, the celebration preserves the balance between past, present, and future. "In the present, the festival commemorates an event or person from the past, with regard to the future: the anamnesis that is so important. Celebrating becomes empty and hollow where ritual reminiscence, representation, and anticipating future prospects fall away. When that happens, the door stands wide open for the anti-festival. Seen from this perspective, festivals and celebrating are always a critical and dangerous game. Christian anamnesis now carries and determines the Christian repertoire of feast days."[10] The explicit expression, the anchoring of the interpersonal relationship in the divine love and faithfulness of union in Christ and his church, belongs to the identity of Christian ritual. In the marriage ceremony we see a sign of God's nearness, a tangible expression of human and divine reality.

The gratuitous also belongs to the dimension of festival as a characteristic of Christian ritual. In that sense, we can't label the marriage ceremony as a magic ritual of making an oath. "Those who want to establish and celebrate their marriage in the church often say that they want to express their thankfulness for the gift of this relationship and in which they recognize divine grace and solicitude. They are resolved to remain faithful to this gift and they are willing to declare this before God and the church community. They also desire to ask God's blessing upon their further life journey."[11]

Marriage as a New Status in the Community

The wedding ceremony confers a new status on the engaged couple. This is expressed as follows in the liturgy:

You have declared your consent before the Church.
May the Lord in his goodness strengthen your consent

and fill you both with his blessings.
What God has joined, men must not divide.

In that sense, the ritual celebration is effective as an active sign of God's grace, as made explicit in the visible, palpable, and audible order of God's promise of love.

The conferral of a new status is a typical characteristic of a rite of passage. The engaged couple makes the transition from unmarried to married "before the church." We cannot deny that in contemporary secular culture, with its anti-institutional and anti-conformist tendencies, marriage is also often regarded as a purely private affair.

> This mutual commitment, whereby self-determination is subjected to actual relativization, must remain a private affair. It cannot be a public matter that the community can sanction. This "feeling of panic" and the mutual challenge in unassailable freedom are already difficult enough in the private sphere without subjecting them to the judging eyes of others. Modern anticonformism thus fits in the individualistic conception of freedom, and in an idea of remaining free.[12]

The philosopher of culture Jacques De Visscher shares the opinion of anthropologists that people are inherently religious and that rituals and religions can be designated as universal and foundational anthropological categories. At the same time, he regards marriage as an institution to be a universal phenomenon. It thus belongs to the fundamental anthropological structures of human existence that orient the human person in his or her perfection, in the manner in which that person hopes to complete his or her existence. Marriage ratifies the end of a certain freedom and awakens expectations that involve mutual obligations from which we may not withdraw.[13] This could be called the negative moment in the rite of passage: the leave-taking from personal freedom and the relativization of one's own freedom to the choice of one's partner. The initiating moment and the promise of a new status are what follow. "Isn't this celebration the symbol *par excellence* that the choice of the partner we desire to be one with is a constitutive moment for our particular course of life as well as for the community, one that reveals our own desires and choice?"[14]

De Visscher also emphasizes the festive character of the celebration:

> The married couple also experiences in the ritual crossing of a new threshold a new birth in which they now, more than ever, can own the words of the baptismal promise: the insight that life is not a self-determined existence but rather a favor, a gift that invites them to *eucháristein*, to thanksgiving, which is best symbolized in the ceremony.[15]

Continuing Questions

I would like to point out that these (postmodern) accents in the inculturation of the marriage liturgy still leave many questions open with regard to the relationship between a generally human religiosity with its rites (of passage) and the particular, uniquely Christian confession of faith about the sacrament of the union that is confirmed in God and Christ. Questions also remain concerning the community of solidarity that institutes this ceremony and, in so doing, maintains it as well. Is the profundity of the uniquely Christian interpretation of the commitment experienced in the communal aspects of the marriage celebration?

On the basis of sociological research into the motivation of young people as to why they want to marry in the church, Liliane Voyé concludes that the great majority, in fact, merely opt for a religious ritual and are hardly concerned with the ecclesial contents and requirements of the marriage as an unbreakable sacrament.[16] She is critical of the too cheaply inflated experience of the religious ritual *(marchandisation)* when only individualistic motives and external pomp are at stake. The religious ritual threatens to become an empty shell, a container without contents and a form without foundation.[17] In order to avoid this there is an urgent need for catechesis and pastoral guidance in the engaged couple's preparations so that their wedding ceremony does not become merely a social, outward sign, but is experienced as an actual symbol of God's union.

Opportunity for Evangelization

Louis-Marie Chauvet also calls for a careful pastoral attitude toward the request for a church wedding.[18] There is an opportunity here for evangelization: a confrontation with the biblical message about marriage. The motives of the engaged couple who request the church ceremony from a latent religiosity or cultural tradition can be explored further in the pastoral conversation. They can be examined for explicitly faith-filled insights into the ecclesial and christological meaning of this symbolic act.

Chauvet speaks of the art of deciphering or decoding the motives in the request *(l'art du décryptage)*, and he shows particular respect for the so-called "religious person with his or her archaisms": this is the humus, the soil in which the seed of the Word can germinate.[19] At the same time, he points out the law of gradations: Is there a certain starting point for faith that can evolve and grow? Such a perspective must remain open in a spirituality of possibility and surprise. By avoiding both rigorism and laxity, the engaged couple's request can be used as a teaching moment toward deeper insight into what their relationship means for themselves as believers in the mystery of Christ and in the church community.

Pastoral guidance can assume the form of initiating, mystagogical catechesis: ushering them into the mystery of Christ. In this way the church is a catechumenal community. The confrontation with the evangelical message will lead to an ethical commitment to experience the marriage in its Christian identity. Then the rite is not merely external *(extériorité)*, but is carried by an inner approval *(intériorité)* of the Christian meaning.[20]

Such pastoral guidance will have to take into account the changed context of contemporary secular culture. In a postmodern presentation of Christian faith, the grand, closed metanarratives and the ideologies no longer enjoy plausibility or legitimacy, and the tradition does not simply continue without further ado. Rather, it opts for the model of an open narrative of the liberating praxis of

Jesus, who appeared to be "interrupting on behalf of God," given the context of the time.[21]

The Open Narrative of Marriage

Lieven Boeve assigns to postmodernity the categories of pluralization and personal identity construction in a narrative structure. Within an inescapably pluralistic context, the believer realizes the particularity of his or her own narrative, which has a threefold structure: (a) a basic attitude of openness to the other: a special sensitivity to that which interrupts (a sensitivity perhaps to be cultivated); (b) the appearance in this openness of the other's witness, and the acknowledgment of the boundaries of one's own narrative; (c) the making operational in a critical praxis of self- and world-critical judgments and actions at the level of making choices.[22] When applied to the mystagogical catechesis of marriage, this could mean that the narrative of each member of the marrying couple is placed in the pattern of Jesus' open narrative during the pastoral conversation. Jesus' narrative then breaks into their respective histories as other, as contrast, as interruption. "Jesus' activity in word and deed functions simultaneously to 'bear witness' as an open narrative. It reflects a non-dominating, *evocative, witness-bearing* approach to language and to the *inexpressible salvific reality* of God."[23]

Boeve points to the evocative power of the parables of the kingdom of God, through which new insights are generated and listeners are challenged to conversion and commitment. The narrative of Jesus' own surrender on the cross is an example of such an open narrative that invites us to conversion and imitation. When such a narrative is invoked, pastoral guidance will open the hearts of the engaged couple to the gratuitous gift that they are able to receive by being married in God's name, when they choose to do so in full awareness. By virtue of their mutual love, they then participate, by means of Jesus' narrative, in an authentic relationship to the mystery of God's love promised in that union.

Against this background, when the faithful have chosen Christian marriage in this manner, the liturgy can indeed be "celebrated" in thanksgiving and festivity. The liturgy itself is not the place for catechesis or moralizing, but it preserves that which is gratuitous and festive in symbol, language, and music, through which the gift in God's name is explicitly expressed to this marrying couple.

Marriage, Secularization, and Radical Pluralism

One last question might be raised in this context: Can the Catholic Church endure with credibility the tension between culture and faith, without the support, which had previously been self-evident, from a now secularized and pluralistic society? If we employ the statistics of participation in church functions as a touchstone or gauge, we cannot deny that the church faces an enormous challenge to become inculturated.

One recent study reveals that the Dutch and Flemish Catholic churches are in a time of transition and fundamental change. Moreover, these developments apply generally across the Western Catholic world.

> What is characteristic of transitional periods is "simultaneous dissimilarity": living simultaneously in that which is being fulfilled and that which is on the way toward something new, the inability to let go and the birth of a new constellation.[24]

The question remains open, but in any case it seems that a special task has been entrusted to catechesis for the future of the church. The catechesis on the sacraments, whose goal is the encounter with God in the liturgical celebration as a condensed moment designed to enlighten Christian life, is rooted in a profound correlation between faith and life that in the dynamic of the biblical message leads to the growth of an adult faith.[25]

The celebration of a church wedding as a sacrament may not stand separately from its engagement in all of life. The mutual promise of love and faithfulness, anchored in God's covenant and in the paschal mystery of Christ with his self-offering as a gift to humanity, opens the perspective of growing together in lifelong faith and attachment. The renewed gift of the Spirit that is invoked and promised over the couple in the wedding liturgy shall remain an inspiration in their lives. In this way, the couple should know that they are carried by God's Spirit of love and faithfulness, which imparts a divine profundity and glimmer to their life together. We see an icon of God's love in the sacrament of marriage: the love of God permeates human love. Such a vision can be the gauge of a lived spirituality of marriage: it is the Holy Spirit, who is poured out anew in the shifting circumstances of married life so that husband and wife can continue to view each other as an icon of God.

With the reversed direction of the gaze, we do not look at God but rather God looks at us through the eyes of the other, as occurs in the icon. In this way, we transcend our subjective center to be in a relation to the other, and we receive ourselves back as the loved one.

God's love in the gift of the Spirit is first. It invites us to enter into this dynamic relationship that is full of love. The one is "gift" to the other in this way, mutually and in one's relationship with God. This is the foundation of God's covenant with humans, of which the marriage covenant is an icon.

In marital love husband and wife see an image of God's love for His people that He sealed with an unbreakable Covenant. Christian married couples believe that God, as Creator and Liberator, has called them 'to be as good as God for one another' so that they may give themselves to each other in a manner reminiscent of Jesus himself. Husband and wife are *sent* to many others, on the basis of their vocation to one another, in order to help them to share in the healing power of their love, just as the ordained office shares the sacrament of marriage in the mission of the Church. Married couples participate in the challenge of being church: growing in union, holiness, catholicity, and apostolicity. Married couples who are believers want to graft their growing union onto God's Covenant. They know themselves to be *sanctified* when they do so, that is to say, close to God and desirous of becoming more and more an 'image of God' to one another.[26]

The eschatological, ultimate destination of the faithful lies in their growth from "image" to "likeness" in the power of the Spirit. The married couple helps to build up the larger *communio* of the church in the nurturing of their family as a house church *(ecclesia domestica)*. In the mutual experience of the gift that they are for each other, they share in the broader experience that is essential to every form of love as an imitation of the unselfish love of Jesus.

Married Love as Evangelical Love

Bishop Paul Schruers describes this experience of mutual love as *the* characteristic of evangelical love:

> Through the love of the one, the latent love of the other blooms and, in turn, becomes a gift to the first. Jesus himself is the ultimate source of this mutual love. Thanks to him, love circulates in the community of his disciples. This is all about the heart of being a disciple, and being disciples together: "This is how all will know that you are my disciples, if you have love for one another" (John 13:35). In that context, Bishop Klaus Hemmerle poses the following question: "To be a gift to one another…isn't that the structural principle of life and the commission of the Church? To make oneself into a gift and to receive the other as a gift, that is the Church's style, its passport."[27]

The subjective desire of the partners is completed by the objectivity of marriage, which enables the couple to rise above their individual potential. A faithful marriage remains a high ideal that is made possible from God's love present in the gift of the Holy Spirit. God himself approaches the married couple and accompanies them on the way where they can be both a gift and a response in continuously renewed creativity and fruitfulness.

Marriage is an enduring task that requires the will to overcome a lack of belief in its own possibilities. The disposition to forgive and the realization that one is always growing are there when the ideal is not always attained. When the married couple dares continuously to let go of the image of the perfect partner and the ideal marriage, choosing with all their heart their actual partner in the changing circumstances of life, then each day is a new beginning in which Christians glimpse God's creative power and nearness with the silent glimmer of the gift of the Spirit.[28]

Ordained Ministry

The Priority of the Divine Calling

The central idea of a postmodern sacramental theology, namely, that we proceed resolutely from the idea of "gift," is obviously applicable to the sacrament of holy orders. Every ordained person is a gift in God's name to the community through the renewed gift of the Spirit. This sacrament is borne by the positive experience of a *call* to service to the community of faith and humanity. The profound mystery of this vocation is distinguished only in accepting that one "is called" to it. The invitation in God's name always comes first.

The process of becoming aware of and acknowledging the invitation develops gradually in the life of an adult believer, who makes a final decision as a response to the gift in the power of the Spirit. In each case, the ordination liturgy for the deacon, priest, and bishop consists in the central text of an explicit *epiclesis* of the Holy Spirit, an invocation of a renewed gift of the Spirit over the ordained to serve in the church, to proclaim the Word, to officiate at the liturgy, and to lead the people of God. In this way, the newly ordained becomes a new person, recreated in the image and likeness of God, in order to serve in the name of Christ. He receives a new *mission* to build up the church by proclaiming Christ and celebrating the sacraments. The nature of the sacrament of ordination is formed by a meaningful triad of call, consecration, and mission.[29]

Scope of the Present Crisis

We cannot simply ignore today's profound crisis in the priesthood. Very few new priests are being ordained. In my opinion, this crisis is a part of a much greater problem, namely, the relationship between the church and the world. So much change in this regard has occurred recently that it is not easy for the priest to find his own place. The priest wants to stand close to the people, among them. He wants to be one of them. Yet, at the same time he is the "man of God" and the "man of the church." He is identified with the church. Since this church exists in a dialectical tension in and against the world, the priest is unavoidably pulled into this field of tension.

Cardinal Godfried Danneels, the primate of Belgium, has expressed the fundamental nature of the question concerning the current priesthood as "the inability to keep one's equilibrium in a field of tension between always paradoxical realities." Is the priesthood temporary, functional, and always to be adapted anew, or does it belong to an everlasting order, standing firm for all time, obedient to the professed church tradition? We must not present this field of tension as if church and world, God and human, were polar opposites. It is about the church *in* the world and God *and* humans at the same time. That is why Cardinal Danneels speaks of the "paradoxical" character of this situation: both poles seem to exclude each other; yet they cannot be thought about apart from each other. The solution to the tension by removing one pole in favor of the other is only an illusory one. Clarification must illuminate the field of tension itself.

Terminological Shifts

At present, an entire series of new words has emerged to replace the prior, classic terms in the literature about the priesthood. This is a question not of fashion but of wishing to nuance the reality in which we find ourselves. Thus, we speak gladly of office (priesthood), the bearer of office (priest), community (parish), members of the community, the office of Peter (papacy), minister (priest in a liturgical gathering), and installation in office (ordination). These terminological alterations are, chiefly, a reaction against a too narrow and cult-conceived image of the priesthood.

Image of the Priest in Changing Cultural Contexts

Vatican II defined the church as a sacrament for the sanctification of the world. The church should make itself known in contemporary society as an active sign and instrument of salvation for today's people. The priest was a different type of figure in a feudal society, for example, from what he was in the ancien régime. He is different in a traditionally democratic order from what he is in a world that is called secular and in which the social self-evidence of faith cannot be presumed. Indeed, this secularization is the strongest challenge to the traditional image of the priesthood. The tension can evolve into a problem because of this. The church of which the priest is the official representative sometimes exhibits too many characteristics of a sacralization that is foreign to this world. And so the priest finds himself in an objective situation of conflict, whether or not he wants it.

Anti-institutional Context of the Post–Vatican II Priest

We have pointed out the anti-institutional tendency of post-modernism. The tension from this attitude can be felt here. An empirical description of priestly ministry as lived by priests ordained since Vatican II reveals the following. In the first place, they are concerned about the preaching, in real life, of the gospel to the people with whom they live, in their regular contact as well as in the administration of the sacraments, which culminates in the celebration of the Eucharist. They attempt to live out their priesthood from two poles: on the one hand, their concern for the life of the community assembled around the Lord (the structural and the official are central here) and, on the other hand, their desire to be (prophetically) inspiring to the people. This is where some discomfort arises in the face of overinstitutionalization in the church, a factor that is experienced as an important constraint in priestly life.

In practice, most priests experience their office as fruitful and united to God, in the degree to which they can actualize their project given this polarization. The sense of fruitfulness and of union with God disappears, however, when they sometimes have to appear to the outside world merely as "clerical" functionaries. The rule that applies to every believer is especially true of the priest: living *in* the world without being *of* the world. It is necessary for the effectiveness of the preaching of the gospel that one be in touch with the contemporary mind-set. This enables the priest to find just the right expression for the self-understanding of the community in which he lives. Yet he knows himself to be called and sent: he feels that he has something to offer this community. He does not identify with the "worldly" community. He remains called and sent to this particular community in order to proclaim Christ's message. This awareness of being sent implies a certain "being-otherwise" within the community. It is necessary to understand this "being-otherwise" precisely so that both the priest himself and the people he serves can give proper attention to this position of separateness without the tension of this "being-otherwise" becoming problematic.

A postmodern sacramental theology outlines the facets of bearing vulnerable witness to the Other in an open narrative and in summoning forth the acknowledgment of the impenetrable mystery of God. The priestly assignment stands out more strongly in its deepest dimension in a postmodern context. This task consists in giving form to one's service to the message of Christ both within and in the face of the Christian community by means of proclamation, liturgy, and leadership. It is not about the person of the priest, but rather about living communities of faith. The priest makes himself unconditionally available to the community: he gives his entire life to it as a gift in the power of the Spirit.

Sociological Insights

Sociological findings confirm these cultural shifts. The priest no longer has to be the only center of the community of faith. According to sociological analyses, the heart of the crisis lies in the loss of status and function of the traditional image of the priest. Priesthood no longer confers greater prestige or the power or esteem that seemed to be self-evident in the past. Now the community of faith incorporates various positions of responsibility. Indeed, this community as such is broken up into smaller groups. The ritual and ethical functions exercised by the priest in established communities in pre-industrial culture wrapped him in a halo of sacredness, implicit prestige, and uncritical acknowledgment. The processes of rationalization, specialization, and secularization have assailed the actual power of priestly expression and privilege in our time. He is in danger of being relegated to the narrow terrain of the religious cult because of this. And precisely now, Vatican

II propels him back into the world as the vulnerable bearer of the Christian message to the heart of the masses and as the leader in the faith to living communities.

The responsibility of leading Christian communities, of which the celebration of the Eucharist is the culminating point, requires a spiritual maturity in faith and a broad human experience that makes it possible to understand a community. At the same time, this requires a group experience that enables the priest to preside over common deliberation within the group and to be a binding element of it.

Sociology and the human sciences have much to teach us about the experience of the priesthood and about the form in which its exercise can be adapted to the needs and requirements of these times. The actual heart of the priesthood reveals itself only for and through faith, and the "science of faith," theology, is therefore called to provide deeper insight. Here I will succinctly mention several models that were drawn up by theologians in order to formulate a theology of the priestly office in the doctrinal context of Vatican II.

Models of Ordained Ministry

Walter Kasper: Charismatic Minister

The model that Walter Kasper developed as a professor in Tübingen places the charisma of community leadership front and center.[30] In his estimation, every theology of the priesthood must depart from the obvious scriptural dictum that there is *only one mediator* between God and humans (1 Tim 2:5) and only one high priest, Jesus Christ (Heb 8:6; 9:15; 12:24). Nevertheless, Jesus is a priest in a special way. He does not line up on the side of the cultic or the sacred in the ancient sense of those terms. Jesus is a priest in his full humanity, and it is precisely there that he is the testimonial sign and bodily form of God's redemptive love. His human surrender to the will of the Father and his service to humanity are the forms in which God's love appears. The work of Christ is proclaimed as surrender to the Father (Heb 7:27; 10:5) and as surrender "for many" (Mark 10:45; 14:24). The ancient cultic and sacrificial concepts are transcended, and the distinction between sacred and profane becomes problematic.

Jesus is a priest in a unique manner. His priesthood, enacted in service and obedience, will exist forever (Heb 9:12; 10:10; 1 Pet 3:18). He is high priest in perpetuity. God and the world are reconciled definitively in his person. A lasting "service of reconciliation" is established in Jesus' unique work of redemption (2 Cor 5:18–20).

The apostolic service that takes place as a response to Christ's commission and in his name is a constitutive element of Christ's own work of salvation. This service is not a supplement or continuation of Jesus' priesthood. It is the historical form of appearance and the organ of the one and only priesthood of Christ. Augustine gives voice to this awareness when he asserts that Christ is the one who baptizes, consecrates, preaches, and leads the church. It follows from this insight that faith in Jesus Christ as Lord is the decisive condition in order to take the priesthood upon oneself. Sharing in his priesthood exists concretely in the obedience of faith and the readiness to serve.

The ecclesiological connection is situated beside the christological motivation, since sharing in Christ's priesthood belongs primarily to the entire church. All Christians form a royal and priestly people, called to proclaim the great deeds of God and to make spiritual sacrifices (1 Pet 2:5–9; Acts 1:6; 5:10). The collective responsibility and the fundamental equality of everyone in the church do not exclude the fact that there exist "varieties of services" (1 Cor 12:5). The conferral of such charisms is summarized in 1 Corinthians 12: 4-20, Romans 12:6-8; and Ephesians 4:11. They are functions that emerge through the Holy Spirit according to the needs of the historical situation.

Thus, the church is not only the apostolic church (built up by the apostles) but also the church of charisms. In Paul's view, charisms are services to the church. Each charism has the church's overall well-being as its goal. Love remains the highest norm (1 Cor 13). The ecclesial office is now founded upon the charism of leadership. The function of that service lies not in plurality but rather in the integration of the various charismatic gifts. The one that confers leadership is responsible for the ordered collaboration and the unity of the other forms of service.

The form of this conferral of service is determined by the principle of sacramental economy, that is to say, the concrete needs and wants of the faithful who are served by that office. The office is essentially a *service to the unity of the church*. Kasper no longer departs from the cultic, sacramental, or consecratory function or from an ontological power of office. He determines the priestly office on the basis of its ecclesial and social function.

Karl Rahner: Proclaimer of the Word

Karl Rahner uses another point of departure in order to determine the enduring essence of the priesthood.[31] He does not start from the sacramental powers that belong exclusively to the priest, nor does he take as his point of departure the concept of mediator. Rather, Rahner begins with the fundamental categories of his theological thought: the church as the sacrament of God's promise of love and the effective character of the "word" in the church.

The church is the sacrament of God's self-promise to the world, which believers accept in faith, hope, and love. The church as so conceived always needs that which we call "office." This office is primarily one, but it can be divided into particular functions that are unique to the church as a socially organized reality.

The church solemnizes its essence as God's self-promise to the world *in the word*, and this word has an eventful, exhibitive, and effective character in principle: that which is proclaimed through this word takes place. The eventful character of this word is gradual and reaches its culmination in what we name *sacrament* in the theological sense of the term. In that sense, according to Rahner, the sacraments are the highest degree of the proclamation of the word.

Once we have entered Karl Rahner's thought-world, we can understand his definition of priest, which he himself calls "recklessly condensed": the priest is the one in relation to a parish, the one who, by order of the church, is the full and therefore official proclaimer of God's Word, to whom is entrusted the sacramentally highest degree of intensity of this Word. Simply put, he is the proclaimer of the gospel in mission and in the name of the church. He fulfills that function in the highest possible realization of that word, namely, in the eucharistic celebration through the anamnesis of the death and resurrection of Christ.

On the basis of Rahner's delineation of the essence of the priesthood, it seems that the priest is not simply a "minister of the cult," and that witnessing to the truly salvific Word of God takes up his entire existence. The proclamation of God's Word as the foundation of priestly ministry immediately gives it a missionary character. From here on it is clear that the priest must always stand in relation to a concrete community, irrespective of whether he encounters it as a Christian community or has to create it himself, and irrespective of how this group is already organized from a sociological perspective. The concrete form of the priestly mission can vary greatly, both ecclesially and sociologically.

Edward Schillebeeckx: Sent by the Lord

Edward Schillebeeckx has developed a detailed theology of the ecclesial office. His fundamental idea is that the office is a visible representation of Christ's *kyrios*-ship: Jesus is the sole Lord and the head of the church. As representative "in the name of Jesus" as head of the church, holders of the ecclesial office have a certain distinction vis-à-vis the body, which Schillebeeckx articulates as "facing the people of God."

Schillebeeckx drafted a nuanced theology of the ecclesial office as an expert at the Second Vatican Council and as a theologian engaged in the analysis of the postconciliar crisis in the priesthood. His starting point is the apostolically ordered community. *Lumen Gentium*, Vatican II's *Dogmatic Constitution on the Church*, deals first with the people of God in its entirety, before taking up the distinction between the faithful and special bearers of office. This was a historic decision: as a result of this sequence the office had to be situated in the context of the service to all the people of God. There are a variety of forms of service in the people of God, but there is a unity of mission.

The leadership form of service is delineated from among the special gifts for the building up of a community of love. The ecclesial offices have the apostolically ordered church community to thank for their origins. The apostles led the community in an authoritative manner from the beginning. Thus, the charism of authority has belonged to the essence of the church from the outset. The Pastoral Letters in the New Testament indicate that the ecclesial office has the special function of answering for the continuity of the faith of the community in relation to the apostolic gospel. The Second Letter of Peter (1:19–21) is an example of this: only the ecclesial office, led by the Holy Spirit, can correctly preserve and properly interpret the doctrine of the apostles.

After the passing of the immediate witnesses to the resurrection, the church situates its apostolic continuity in the ecclesial office. According to the New Testament, this ecclesial office is representative of apostolic authority in two characteristics. Although a part of the community, the church leader as such nevertheless also stands *apart from the community*. He exercises his authority as *sent from the Lord* and as a service of love to the community. His authority is also the service of Christ: "on behalf of Christ" (2 Cor 5:20). The official leader has to ensure that Christ is indeed the sole lord, priest, and leader of the redeemed community.

The meaning and contents of the priestly office are naturally determined by the unique essence and mission of the entire church. Schillebeeckx schematizes the powers of the office in the following manner: leading and accompanying Christian life in the community; taking the lead in service to the word in faithfulness to the apostolic confession of faith; presiding over the sacramental celebrations; exercising concern for evangelical consolation and encouragement; setting an example of love; guaranteeing the evangelical concern that the Christian community must have for every person, something that is critical of society and sometimes also the church. Finally, the welcoming of new candidates to the priesthood also belongs to the normal duties of community leadership. The church leadership must guarantee in loving service that Christ is acknowledged as the sole Lord of the community.[32]

The New Contribution of Vatican II

We find the heart of Vatican II's doctrine on the priesthood in article 2 of the *Decree on the Ministry and Life of Priests*

(*Presbyterorum Ordinis*, December 7, 1965). The point of departure is the entire people of God, which has become a royal priesthood in Christ. Every Christian is anointed by the Holy Spirit and shares in the sanctification and mission of Christ himself.

> So it was that Christ sent the apostles just as He Himself had been sent by the Father. Through these same apostles He made their successors, the bishops, sharers in his consecration and mission. Their ministerial role has been handed down to priests in a limited degree. Thus established in the order of the priesthood, they are co-workers of the episcopal order in the proper fulfillment of the apostolic mission entrusted to the latter order by Christ.
>
> Inasmuch as it is connected with the episcopal order, the priestly office shares in the authority by which Christ Himself builds up, sanctifies, and rules His Body. Therefore, while it indeed presupposes the sacraments of initiation, the sacerdotal office of priests is conferred by that special sacrament through which priests, by the anointing of the Holy Spirit, are marked with a special character and are so configured to Christ the Priest that they can act in the person of Christ the Head.

Holy Orders is a separate sacrament with its own specific grace and sign. It is a grace for the mission that the priest is to fulfill. By sign we mean a special participation in Christ's priesthood in order to act in the person of Christ the Head (*in persona Christi Capitis*). Whereas Trent called upon the powers of consecration and absolution in order to distinguish the uniqueness of the priesthood from the rest of the faithful, the distinction is clarified here by pointing out the sacrament of the *Ordo* that is directed toward the mission. Priesthood as a sacrament is a free gift of God through a special gift of the Spirit. In order to characterize this gift, the council decree appeals to the formulation: conformity to Christ's priesthood in order to act as the *Head* of and for (in favor of) the body. As fellow workers of the bishops, priests represent this function as head in leading the church community.

This is where the new contribution of Vatican II relates to the doctrine of Trent, which determined the uniqueness of the priesthood on the basis of sacramental power. This is an ecclesiological and christological definition: in everything that priests do in virtue of their office, they are united with Christ for the building up of his body, the church community. Priesthood is a sacrament and the active symbol of Christ as head of the church. This is the immediate basis for the extensiveness of the priestly function: it is universal in principle. This is described further in the next paragraph in the decree, in which the content of the ministerial priesthood is defined not only in relation to its cultic function but also in relation to the entire apostolic mission: the whole work of proclamation and building up the church, issuing in and proceeding from the Eucharist, completion and new source of grace, as the highest celebration of Christ's mystery of redemption.

Saint Paul already conceived of this proclamation as a "liturgy," but as the cult of the new covenant (Rom 15:16; 12:1), in which Christ is the sole mediator. Priestly service proceeds from the Gospels, draws its power from the paschal mystery, and stands ready for the final judgment, where God's glory will become visible.

In the context of the classical vision of priestly life in a separate clerical state, we must say that the council accentuates an actual presence in today's world. This is necessary so that he might "be of real service to people" without conforming himself to the world at the expense of the witnessing power of his entire life. This tension is a life-sized task for every Christian and *a fortiori* for the priest. The classical spirituality of the priesthood was informed by the vision of the priest as an *alter Christus*, an "other" Christ, on the basis of his conformity to Christ as signified and realized through the sacrament. Without doubt, this form of symbolization remains powerful in a postmodern approach.[33]

The symbolic character of the function of the priest rests on the parallel between the relationship of Jesus to his group of disciples on the one hand, and of the priest to his faithful, on the other. In the case of the priest, this function extends to all of life and all pastoral tasks, but it receives its strongest expression in presiding over the liturgy. It is characteristic of a sign that it bears a likeness to, and reveals or unveils something of, the thing signified; but it is unique to the symbol that there is also some dissimilarity, and thus distance from and veiling of what it signifies. Human acceptance and recognition are involved in the priest's role as Christ's representative as head of the church community: the priest is called to prove in his life that he may act "in the name of Christ." This is an existential challenge to which he devotes his life, because he also experiences in his heart that he "is only human" and that he functions simultaneously as a revealer and concealer in the order of the sacramental symbol. He also experiences the "distance" between the sign and its signification.

The sacrament of ordination, as a new gift of the Spirit, confers upon the priest a new status that he receives from within the church community. This new status identifies him as charged with the threefold task of proclamation, sanctification, and leadership. Vatican II resolutely opted to replace the earlier image of the priesthood with an "apostolic" image.

The mission of the priest is universal and covers his entire life. The task of proclamation, although not separated from the task of sanctification, enjoys a certain priority. There is still some friction between the sacred, cultic image of the priesthood and the image that arises from the awareness of mission. Monsignor Albert Dondeyne characterizes this as follows: "As a unity of religious meaning, the priestly vocation is an apostolic and ecclesial call in its most profound essence or, in other words, a total giving of one's life, in response to a divine call, to God and to the Church for the salvific work of God."[34]

Joseph Ratzinger also called upon the notion of vocation and mission in order to delineate the uniqueness of the priestly office. He characterizes being a priest as an apostolic existence. Just as Jesus himself fulfilled his mission, the Christian priesthood is founded on being called to the mission of Jesus and being sent together with him.[35] Gisbert Greshake, in his theology of the priesthood, attaches great importance to priestly spirituality; theology is incomplete without spirituality.[36] Representing "in the name of Christ" must go together with representing "in the name of the church" *(in persona ecclesiae totius)*. Alongside the christological foundation, Greshake also develops an ecclesial-pneumatological foundation of the office and places it ultimately in a trinitarian perspective. Just as Jesus was sent by the Father, the priest is sent in order to show the Father. The office lies at the crossroads of *auctoritas Christi* and *communio* of the Holy Spirit. The priest can be the instrument of Christ today in the power of the Spirit, specifically by being integrated with the representation of Christ that happens in and through every believer on the basis of the common priesthood. *Communio* is the ultimate goal.[37]

Ordained Ministry as Service

In its most profound reality, the priesthood is characterized as a *service*, a *diakonia* in imitation of Christ's priestly service: service to God first, then also service to Christ, service to the church community and ultimately to the world. In fact, it is about service to the reality of Christ in the community.[38] The unique grace of the priesthood is a *gratia pro aliis:* a gift that is for the good of the community.

People are called to this service, ordained and sent through the mediation of the church. The religious meaning is available and intelligible only from within a position of faith. The devotion to Christ the high priest and conformity to him occur through the gift of the Spirit, which is truly communicated in the laying on of hands. By this means the ordained person—the permanent deacon, priest, or bishop—is taken up in the collegiality and mutual service of office in order to build up the church through the proclamation of the gospel. He shares in Christ's mission for the eschatological service of redemption (2 Cor 5:18–20). In the Christian community, he is the ongoing sign of Christ's saving presence. His apostolic service is a gift of the life-giving Spirit: the ordained individual is "equipped with hope," rendered fit "to be a servant of a new covenant," directed toward the final fulfillment that surpasses everything. The priest serves the re-creation of the person into a greater likeness with the image of God. He fulfills this service by openly proclaiming the truth, Christ Jesus, the sole Lord (2 Cor 3:4–4:6). As such he is an icon of the invisible Christ.

Chapter Ten

ECUMENICAL PERSPECTIVES

He is the "icon" of the invisible God,
the firstborn of all creation;
for in him all things in heaven and on earth were created,
things visible and invisible,
whether thrones or dominions or rulers or powers—
all things have been created through him and for him.
He himself is before all things,
and in him all things hold together.

He is the head of the body, the church;
he is the beginning, the firstborn from the dead,
so that he might come to have first place in everything.
For in him all the fullness of God was pleased to dwell,
and through him God was pleased to reconcile to himself
    all things,
whether on earth or in heaven,
by making peace through the blood of his cross.

(Colossians 1:15–20)

Sacraments are acts in and of the church community; they came into being and were developed in time as forms of the continuation of and participation in Christ, the primordial sacrament. They are human actions in imitation of the will of Christ, as they were conceived in the interpretation of church leadership under the inspiration of the Holy Spirit. The concrete expression of the seven sacraments is certainly joined to the last will of Christ, who entrusted the redemptive work of reconciliation to the church. We have thus characterized the church as the basic sacrament in which the seven sacraments have unfolded in time, with shifting forms but faithful to a sense and direction that were willed by Christ. In our postmodern reformulation of the classical proposition that all seven were instituted by Christ, we are quite aware that the seven sacraments developed historically.

The Roman Catholic Church is engaged in ecumenical dialogue in order to support Christian witnessing to the world. The separation among the Christian churches remains a source of scandal. Mutual forms of recognition are important steps on the pilgrimage toward unity. The notion of seven sacraments remains particularly difficult for the churches that came into existence during the sixteenth-century Reformation. In general, these churches acknowledge only the two sacraments of baptism and Last Supper because, in their estimation, these two are clearly supported by scripture.

Karl Rahner was of the opinion that we need not simply abandon the seven sacraments in our ecumenical talks. They came into being in a historical development, led by the Holy Spirit. On the basis of good insight into this historical evolution, and using his definition of sacrament as the highest degree of the proclamation of the Word, Rahner means that the seven sacraments can continue to be a treasure in a reconciled diversity.

Postmodernity and Sacramental Ecumenicity

Postmodern sacramental theology distances itself from the hylemorphistic *(materia–forma)* structure of the sacraments as instruments, and from scholastic thought in the categories of cause *(causa)* and effect. To some extent, the other churches can consent to and approve of the new view of and approach to the sacraments as dynamic gifts of the Spirit and as the language of the self-giving God. It is not difficult to recognize that sacraments are acts of prayer in the first place, invocations *(epiclesis)* of the Holy Spirit, to which we respond in faith. The emphasis on the community of faith, as highlighted in a postmodern perspective, can also help us to avoid viewing the sacraments as an individualistic means of receiving grace in a clerical context. Sacraments are prayers in the church community where we receive our identity. As such, the sacraments indeed delimit the church community. Certainly, in the celebration of the sacraments of initiation we belong to the church community by means of these sacraments.

Continuing Gaps and Elements of Communion

Sacraments show the boundaries of the church—that is, they reveal both difference and shared faith. For example, the believer belongs to the church community in which he or she was baptized. Christian baptism in the name of Jesus is mutually recognized and, in and of itself, forms no hindrance to ecumenical dialogue. There is a far-reaching accord over the legitimacy of infant baptism on the condition that it is accompanied by good catechesis that supports the further commitment of Christian parents. In this way, the gap is bridged between a baptism of confession (adult baptism) and infant baptism.

Again, the Catholic Church clearly accepts that the gift of the Holy Spirit takes place in baptism. The difference that has grown in the Western tradition by creating a separate celebration for confirmation and thereby dividing the process of initiation does not detract from the initial gift of the Holy Spirit in baptism. The recognition of baptism as the sacrament of the beginning of Christian life allows for yet further ceremonial steps to accompany growth in this Christian life. We agree that baptism, as administered in the Christian churches, initiates one into the mystery of Christ and establishes a relation to the holy Trinity. The divergence occurs when we consider into which church one is being initiated.

Hindrances remain in the conception of the ecclesial office, acting *in persona Christi Capitis*, in the interpretation of the sacrificial character of the Eucharist and the real presence *(realis praesentia)*. Here the Catholic view continues to embrace the explanation of transubstantiation as formulated by scholastic (Aristotelian) theology, as the most profound statement of the miraculous transformation—*mirabilis conversio*—of bread and wine into the body and blood of our Lord Jesus Christ.[1]

The unity among the various churches will not take place on an organizational level, but rather as a conciliar community in

119

mutual dialogue and communication, whereby unity in reconciled difference can be mutually acknowledged on the basis of the New Testament understanding of *koinōnia, communio*. One theologian regards *koinōnia* not as the final blueprint for the reconstruction of the church community,[2] but as the horizon toward which the churches develop. However, the fact that we can see this horizon already decreases the distance between the churches, so that the community that is already oriented toward mutual reconciliation comes into view. This perspective clarifies the title of his book, *Pilgrims on the Way*, whereby figures such as Abraham and Moses, who journeyed as nomads, and a figure such as Cleophas and his traveling companion on the road to Emmaus—initially dejected disciples who later come to recognition—can serve as examples of the pilgrimage that is now occurring in the Christian churches.

We are also reminded of figures such as the ecumenically minded Patriarch Athenagoras and Pope Paul VI, who embraced one another on January 5, 1964, in Jerusalem in mutual recognition of their faith. One scholar of ecumenism recalls the older ecumenical literature that still spoke of the "reunion of the churches" (understood as a universal church, led by Rome, from which the other confessions have dissociated themselves), and in fact relativizes every model of "unity in reconciled difference" or conciliation,

> if Christians do not succeed in understanding the churches in which they have received the faith simply as the places in which they have heard the message of God's irrevocable and unconditional Yes to men and women in Jesus Christ, a word of God to all people, on which they can rely in life and death. It is not the churches that are the goal and content of faith, but the living God. The churches have to withdraw before him....[3]

In the same article, I was struck by the reference to the speech of Patriarch Athenagoras in 1964: "When asked by a reporter from the French Roman Catholic journal *La Croix*, 'Do you believe that there will soon be reunion with the Roman Church?,' Athenagoras replied: 'We were never united.' He then went on to tell the astonished questioner: 'We lived together in fellowship and we will continue to live in fellowship.'"[4]

This point of view expresses how the future of the ecumenical movement can be delineated further. Just as the doctrine on justification is no longer a divisive factor, so should the same be true of the celebration of the sacraments. Even if the other churches do not recognize the seven sacraments per se, such sacramental celebrations provide the opportunity for prayer, confession of faith (confirmation), consolation (penance and anointing of the sick), blessing (marriage), and ordination (priesthood). In the final analysis of the eschatological dimension, the kingdom of God comes first, not in a chronologically distant future, but as the current dimension in which that which is definitive in the surrender of faith is experienced with its final result. Armed with four differing approaches that ecumenist Anton Houtepen offers us,[5] we can make the transition to the treatment of postmodernity as a new philosophical and cultural framework in which faith in the message of the sole Lord Jesus can be directed to the world.

Houtepen's Approach

Houtepen begins by using the results of historical research to reconstruct the rupture lines of the past and to reevaluate their truth ("to overcome history by history"): this must certainly happen, and, in such an investigation, difficult elements can be eliminated. A second step is the model, already discussed, of unity in reconciled difference. But Houtepen goes even further, returning to the time before the rupture, to the source in Jesus Christ and the Spirit. Finally, he describes that "which proceeds from a dynamically continuous but at the same time eschatologically open tradition".[6] This is supported by Paul Ricoeur's hermeneutics (*Time and Narrative*), in which the conferral of meaning on facts from the past does not become reduced to a subjective construction. On the contrary, Ricoeur starts out from a *préfiguré*, something that is sketched in reality itself, that forms the basis for a ground plan, our narrative *configuration* within which we communicate with ourselves. "This narrative form—our story about the facts—is never the goal in and of itself: it aims at the *réfiguration* of the one being addressed, the spectator or listener: it wants to accomplish something, namely a change in thought, a turning around, a conversion."[7]

We can agree with Houtepen and Vercruysse that aspiring to ecumenical consensus belongs to the great dreams of modernity, the rational control over all of reality and its signification. This form of unity could be characterized as a modern "grand meta-narrative," a form of ideology and dogmatizing that was unmasked by Enlightenment thinkers and the masters of suspicion. Society is moving toward a radical plurality of opinion, described by Jean-Francois Lyotard as *"la condition postmoderne."* Thought by consensus is not an appropriate way of doing justice to the difference *(le différend)* that lies at the foundation of confessional divergences.

Marion's Icon

Where Ricoeur still preserved an ontological point of reference, Jean-Luc Marion's book *God Without Being (Dieu sans l'être)* relativizes thought that rests on ontological categories in valid discourse about the God of revelation.[8] As a philosopher, Marion offers his phenomenological vision of a theology that is degraded to idolatry when it thinks and speaks in ontological terms about God. Then God becomes an idol, an image of God that is thought and projected by the subject.

Using a magisterial and inimitable play on words between idol and icon, he refers real thought about God to the biblical revelation with the purely gratuitous gift of God's love *(agapē/charité)* in God's highest icon, the man Jesus, as its culminating point. Marion sees the Eucharist as the "site," the place *par excellence* where justice can be done to the true God: God gave himself unselfishly in the gift of Christ *(abandon,* surrender). Marion treats the theme of real presence using the character of gift, with the play on the words *présent* and *don,* in English translation "the present and the gift." Here and now it is simply as gift that the real presence can be understood. Yet Marion preserves the word *transubstantiation* for this gift of Christ to the faithful as a proper term, understandable because the exercise of one's thought is necessary in order to take up a hermeneutic of distance so as to recognize the difference between the visible form *(l'apparence)* and the reality that is present and received.

The gifts become transparent as icons before the *agapē* of God and Christ. The believer is *l'adonné*, to whom the gift is gratuitously given. The real relationship with God takes place in this objective space of being-given, *Étant donné*, the title of Marion's other work as *An Essay of a Phenomenology of Givenness.*[9]

The church is built up as the Mystical Body of Christ through the Eucharist. In my estimation Marion's vision, with its central concepts of icon and gift, can offer an opening to opportunities for the development of a sacramental theology in which the accent is no longer on *cause*, but rather on a very personal and grateful relation to the true God whom we meet among the community of faith, the body of Christ, who reveals and offers us the true God. The response to this offer is prayer, surrender, and contemplation.

Chauvet and the Symbol

Chauvet's sacramental theology also emphasizes the personalistic and communitarian character of the encounter with God in the experience of the sacraments. His central idea is *"parole de Dieu au risque du corps,"* the word of God at the mercy of the body.[10]

Chauvet makes historical distinctions between the era of objective thought about God (onto-theology) and subjective, modern thought, only to arrive at a radical thought in terms of symbol. A network of symbols is established by the sacraments, *"un réseau symbolique, un ordre symbolique,"* in which human life becomes integrated into participation in divine life. Chauvet attaches great importance to the anthropological dimension of the sacraments: the sacraments are grand rituals of life in which all religions endeavor to express a relation to the transcendent. It is important to note that Chauvet insists strongly on the evangelization of such rites of passage in order to avoid (as does Marion) projecting the needs of the *homo religiosus* too subjectively and unjustly onto these forms of expression that indeed exhibit universal characteristics. The role of the witnessing community is particularly important here. The special, open narrative of God's revelation in the man Jesus, in his body—not as an ideological grand metanarrative—with his death and resurrection as the heart of the message, is experienced further in the Christian community that is also called the "body of Christ."

Chauvet's postmodern theology also contains good starting points for the development of an applied, unhegemonistically conceived sacramental theology for our time. And he also believes that ritual behavior must, in any case, be supplemented and corrected by authentically realistic, ethical stakes. A communal conception of the sacraments could be acknowledged in this way, in which the accent on the symbolic and eschatological aspects is accompanied by the soteriological and ecclesiological aspects.

Ecumenist Martien Brinkman has sketched the main lines of such a communal understanding of the sacraments: "The critical social role of the celebration of the sacraments is expressed in the eschatological aspect. The symbolic aspect is more concerned with the community-founding dimension of the sacrament as a ritual."[11]

Dialoging with Postmodernity, Not Postmodernism

In my opinion, we can let go of our initial skepticism about the postmodern framework. This skepticism had to do with Jacques Derrida's philosophy of deconstruction, which formed the basis of postmodern thought and was often misunderstood as *démolition*. Derrida aimed at a reconstruction after critically weighing the preceding theories, which he regarded not as a heap of ruins but rather as building blocks for a new construction. The skepticism also had to do with Martin Heidegger's atheistic phenomenology, which emphasizes the inadequacy of metaphysical conceptual categories to recover the identity of God.

There is always a distance from the unspeakable mystery of God, an absence within the presence. A postmodern sacramental theology is attentive to this difference. It replaces a concentration on presence or identity with an emphasis on the difference between what we say in performative speech about God and

Christ—who are experienced as present or absent in the celebration of the sacraments—and the real encounter with God.

We can make a connection here not only with representing to ourselves the presence of Christ in the eucharistic gift but also with the conception of the priest who acts as representative of Christ, the head. A postmodern vision holds us back from strongly emphasizing the presence of or the identity with Christ. The symbolic character must be radically extended here in the direction of icons and transparence. Stanislas Breton speaks of "traces" in his book *Écriture et révélation* (where Chauvet finds much of his philosophy of language): *"les traces"* of God's presence. The traces remain in the history of God's revelation in Jesus Christ and in the community; traces as signs of remembrance *(memorials)* that put us on our way and direct us toward eschatological fulfillment. *Traces* can also be translated as scars, signs of being hurt from wounds of the past, something that is sometimes painfully experienced in ecumenical dialogue, and from which we can learn for the future.

Thus, it is important to acknowledge the traces of God's action in the other churches by a movement of empathy that allows the other churches to be fully "other," without seeking to chain them or stifle them. A new paradigm of universality has been proposed in which mutual interconnectedness is expressed in actual *diakonia* through collective ethical witnessing with regard to the world. The role of sacramental celebration exists, then, in the unpretentious, vulnerable witnessing as *anamnesis, memoria passionis* (J. B. Metz), in the remembrance of the death and resurrection of the Lord Jesus, in the grateful praise of God in the doxology, in the unbroken invocation of the Holy Spirit in the *epiclesis*, and in sincere intercessory prayers, the *intercessio*. This liturgy is meant to bring about conversion and readiness for service.

True service can lead to a renewed, transparent experience of church, in combination with a well-considered, detailed concept of *diakonia*. In the profane literature dating from the time of the redaction of the New Testament, this term *diakonia* did not only mean lowly servitude, waiting on tables, as is mostly thought nowadays; rather, as uncovered by J. N. Collins's exegetical studies, it also conveyed the image of authoritatively acting in the name of the one who has given you a mission, a form of recognized mediation and proclamation "in the name of," a real representation. When applied to the ecclesial forms of office, this *diakonia* therefore receives a new recognition in service to the gospel.[13]

Finally, how will the ecumenical community appear in the context of postmodernity? "Will the ecumene become a deconstruction of confessional traditions and a reconstruction with elements of diverse origin? Or will the accent fall upon praxis in becoming transparent before the Secret that is sacramentally present and active among us in the plurality of ecclesial life?"[14] Whoever perceives the guiding power that is active in the "white between the lines" or in the silence, the interval between consecutive events, knows that the answer lies in the second of these two alternatives. But it remains a challenge.

In my opinion, the ecumenical movement will develop further in open communication with a robust invitation to conversion and reconciliation: reconciliation as meant in the Hebrew *kippēr*, which originally meant "to iron the creases," to preserve the creases in the entire cloth: the creases must not disappear as disturbing elements; rather, they set off and decorate the one fabric.

All Christian churches come forth from the one Christ event. If we express the current plurality of churches with this metaphor of a cloth, a fabric, a context, then it is about preserving the entire cloth in all its beauty, to heal the rift through reconciliation. This is the way of pilgrimage that has been pointed out, to which Johann Reikerstorfer also points in the conclusion of his article about a new paradigm of universality. It is, namely, that we cannot consign difference, the nonidentical, to an abstract intellectual universalism (Enlightenment—modernity), but that the "other," the Other, is to be recognized as a subject in the *memoria passionis.*

> Taking seriously the memory of suffering opens a promising perspective for Christian discourse about God in the time of postmodern splintering. Perhaps it can then become the public sign of the not to be silenced theme of God in a time of plurality and difference. In this ecumene, an ecumene of *empathy*, the great religions would be able to come closer together, productively taking part in giving form to a new, worldwide society.[15]

126

EPILOGUE

The familiar Christian hymn "Veni Creator Spiritus" offers inspiration and insight as we conclude these thoughts on sacraments and postmodernity. This hymn of praise could be sung for every sacrament as the musical setting of the entire celebration, the language of the self-giving God.

> Come, Holy Spirit, creator, come
> From your bright heavenly throne,
> Come take possession of our souls
> And make them all your own.
>
> You who are called Paraclete
> Blest gift of God above,
> The living spring, the living fire,
> Sweet unction and true love.
>
> You who are sevenfold in your grace,
> Finger of God's right hand;
> His promise, teaching little ones
> To speak and understand.
>
> O guide our minds with your blest light;
> With love our hearts inflame;
> And with strength, which never decays,
> Confirm our mortal frame.
>
> Far from us drive our deadly foe;
> True peace unto us bring;
> And through perils, lead us safe
> Beneath your sacred wing.

Through you may we the Father know;
Through you the eternal Son,
And you the Spirit of them both,
Thrice-blessed Three in One.

All glory to the Father be,
With his co-equal Son;
The same to you, great Paraclete,
While endless ages run.
Amen.

NOTES

Chapter 1: Life Rituals

1. Edward Schillebeeckx, "Naar een herontdekking van de christelijke sacramenten. Ritualisering van religieuze momenten in het alledaagse leven," *Tijdschrift voor Theologie* 40 (2000): 164–87, esp. 171 and 183.

2. Johann Wolfgang van Goethe, as cited in Otto Semmelroth, *Church and Sacrament*, trans. Emily Schossberger (Notre Dame, IN: Fides, 1965), 61–62.

3. Ibid., 67 [translator's note].

4. Edward Schillebeeckx, *Theologisch testament: Notarieel nog niet verleden* (Baarn: Uitgeverij H. Nelissen, 1994), 190.

5. Lambert Leijssen, Michel Cloet, and Karel Dobbelaere, eds., *Levensrituelen: Geboorte en doopsel*, Kadoc-studies 20 (Leuven: Universitaire Pers Leuven, 1996), 7. See also in this series: Kadoc-studies 12, *Het vormsel* (1991) and Kadoc-studies 24, *Het huwelijk* (2000). The center may be contacted at Kadoc: Catholic Documentation and Research Center, Vlamingenstraat 39, B-3000 Leuven, Belgium.

6. Paul Post and Lambert Leijssen, "Huwelijksliturgie: inculturatie van een levensfeest," in *Levensrituelen: Het huwelijk*, Kadoc-studies 24 (Leuven: Universitaire Pers Leuven, 2000), 179–96.

7. See Veerle Draulans and Henk Witte, "Initiatie in de vrijwilligerskerk: Verkenningen in vergelijkend perspectief," in *De kerk in Vlaanderen: avond of dageraad?*, ed. Lieven Boeve (Leuven: Davidsfonds, 1999), 167–88.

8. Jozef De Kesel, *Omwille van zijn Naam: Een tegendraads pleidooi voor de kerk* (Tielt: Lannoo, 1994), 155 and 152. See my further observations on this issue: Lambert Leijssen, "Sacramentologische reflectie op het kinderdoopsel," in *Levensrituelen: Geboorte en Doopsel*, 261–77, esp. 271–72.

9. Guido Vanheeswijck, *Tussen afbraak en opbouw: Christendom in een postmoderne tijd. Moeilijkheden en mogelijkheden* (Averbode: Altiora, 1997), 43–46.

10. Jacques De Visscher, *Een te voltooien leven: Over rituelen van de moderne mens* (Kapellen: Uitgeverij Pelckmans; Kampen: Kok Agora, 1996), 187: "We suspect that even the secular-modern individual witnesses gaps in the technological worldview, experiences festivity only by way of metaphorization, and is unable to articulate the enigmatic without symbolization during crucial moments in the course of life (birth, marriage, festivals, in distinguishing guilt and alienation, in the face of death). We also think that this modern individual cannot be entirely alienated from his or her attitude toward the sacred because this attitude is a fundamental anthropological category. He or she moves in a religious-symbolic vacuum because he or she is so out of touch with the traditional Christian forms of the sacred, yet appreciates them as exotic or aesthetically pleasing because they still call forth the foundational in one way or another." About De Visscher's phenomenological analysis in confrontation with Paul Moyaert's vision, see Piet Raes, "Over maat en mateloosheid: Jacques De Visscher en de zin van rituelen, symbolen en lijfelijkheid," *Streven* 68 (2001): 699–707. See also "Rituelen en religie," *Kultuurleven* 64, no. 6 (1997): De Visscher's book is discussed by Stijn Van den Bossche (pp. 108–11); see also Jacques De Visscher's contribution, "Rituelen in een seculiere cultuur" (pp. 16–23); and the dialogue, Lambert Leijssen, Paul Moyaert, and Lieven Boeve, "Rituelen, sacramenten en liturgieën" (pp. 5–15).

11. Jacques De Visscher, "Geherbergd in een traditie: Symbolen en rituelen dienen tot niets," *Tijdschrift voor Geestelijk Leven* 54 (1998): 121. This issue offers an idiosyncratic account of the Youth Pastoral Days (1997) under the title *Breekbaar als glas: Over de broosheid van symbolen en riten.* See herein the contributions of Jan Dumon, "Het einde van de christelijke liturgie in het Westen?" (pp. 123–34); and Marianne Merckx, "De kracht van de broosheid: De sacramentaliteit van het alledaagse leven" (pp. 135–47).

12. Gerard Lukken, *Rituals in Abundance: Critical Reflections on the Place, Form and Identity of Christian Ritual in Our Culture,* Liturgia condenda 17 (Leuven/Dudley, MA: Peeters, 2005).

13. Ibid., 385.

14. Bert Claerhout, "God in Frankrijk," *Tertio* 100 (January 9, 2002): 2.

15. Ibid. The bishop was Gerard Defois, Bishop of Lille.

Chapter 2: New Visions in Sacramental Theology

1. See Lambert Leijssen, "Christus als oersacrament: Bijbelse benadering en liturgische vormgeving," in *"De mens leeft niet van brood alleen…": Leven van symbolen en sacramenten*, Nikè-reeks 16, ed. Lambert Leijssen (Leuven/Amersfoort: Acco, 1987), 133–53.

2. Erik Borgman, *Edward Schillebeeckx: een theoloog in zijn geschiedenis. Deel 1: Een katholieke cultuurtheologie (1914-1965)* (Baarn: Uitgeverij H. Nelissen, 1999), 289.

3. Ibid., 249–50.

4. Ibid., 238 n. 18. Concerning the simultaneous developments in the visions of Schillebeeckx, Rahner, and Semmelroth, see p. 250 n. 50.

5. See Lambert J. Leijssen, "Rahner's Contribution to the Renewal of Sacramentology," *Philosophy & Theology* 9 (1995): 201–22.

6. Lieven Boeve, "Apocalyptiek als onontkoombare actuele theologische denkfiguur," in *God ondergronds: Opstellen voor een theologisch vrijdenker. Aangeboden aan Professor Georges De Schrijver*, ed. Lieven Boeve and Jacques Haers (Averbode: Altiora, 2001), 389, with reference to "Eschatology" in Karl Rahner and Herbert Vorgrimler, *Theological Dictionary*, trans. Richard Strachan (New York: Herder and Herder, 1965), 149.

7. See Lambert Leijssen et al., *L'Esprit Saint et la liturgie*, Textes et Études Liturgiques 9 (Leuven: Abbaye du Mont César, 1986), 3–8, 77–80.

8. Antoon Vergote, *Het huis is nooit af: Gedachten over mens en religie* (Antwerpen/Utrecht: De Nederlandsche Boekhandel, 1974), 227–51. See Lambert Leijssen, "De eucharistievierende gemeenschap als een gemeenschap van handelende personen," *Tijdschrift voor liturgie* 67 (1983): 39–60.

9. Antoon Vergote, "De cultus als werkzame geloofsuitdrukking," in *Het huis is nooit af*, 107–33.

10. Ibid., 129.

11. Piet Fransen, "Modellen in de theologie van de sacramenten," *Collationes* 12 (1982): 131–55; and idem, "De sacramenten als gemeenschapsviering van de goddelijke mysteries: Een model voor onze tijd?" *Collationes* 13 (1983): 139–63. See also Piet Fransen, "Sacraments as Celebrations," in idem, *Hermeneutics of the Councils and Other Studies*, Bibliotheca Ephemeridum Theologicarum Lovaniensium 69 (Leuven: University Press/Uitgeverij Peeters, 1985), 436–55.

12. Robert Pannet, *Le catholicisme populaire: 30 ans après "La France, pays de mission?"* (Paris: Centurion, 1974).

13. George S. Worgul, Jr., *From Magic to Metaphor: A Validation of Christian Sacraments* (New York/Ramsey, NJ: Paulist Press, 1980).

14. Louis-Marie Chauvet, *Symbol and Sacrament: A Sacramental Reinterpretation of Christian Existence*, trans. Patrick Madigan and Madeleine Beaumont (Collegeville, MN: Liturgical Press, 1995); and idem, *The Sacraments: The Word of God at the Mercy of the Body* (Collegeville, MN: Liturgical Press, 2001).

15. Francisco Taborda, *Sakramente: Praxis und Fest*, Bibliothek Theologie der Befreiung. Die Kirche, Sakrament der Befreiung, trans. Horst Goldstein (Düsseldorf: Patmos, 1988).

16. Leonardo Boff, *Sacraments of Life: Life of the Sacraments*, trans. John Drury (Beltsville, MD: Pastoral Press, 1987).

Chapter 3: The Seven Sacraments

1. Leonardo Boff, *Sacraments of Life: Life of the Sacraments*, trans. John Drury (Beltsville, MD: Pastoral Press, 1987), 57–58.

2. Pope Paul VI, *Divinae Consortium Naturae* (August 15, 1971).

3. *Catechism of the Catholic Church* (Liguori, MO: Liguori Publications, 1994), 311, no. 1210.

4. Louis-Marie Chauvet, *Symbol and Sacrament: A Sacramental Reinterpretation of Christian Existence*, trans. Patrick Madigan and Madeleine Beaumont (Collegeville, MN: Liturgical Press, 2001), 157.

5. See Paul Post and Lambert Leijssen, "Huwelijksliturgie: inculturatie van een levensfeest," in *Levensrituelen. Het huwelijk*, Kadoc-studies 24, ed. Roger Burggraeve, Michel Cloet, Karel Dobbelaere and Lambert Leijssen (Leuven: Universitaire Pers Leuven, 2000), 190–91.

Chapter 4: Sacramental Presence in a Postmodern Context

1. See Guido Vanheeswijck, *Tussen afbraak en opbouw: Christendom in een post-moderne tijd. Moeilijkheden en mogelijkheden* (Averbode/Ten Have: Altiora, 1997), 14–18.

Notes

2. Catherine Cornette and Kristiaan Depoortere, *Fragmenten: Postmoderniteit en theologie*, Nike-reeks 29 (Leuven: Acco, 1993), 5.

3. Lieven Boeve, "Erfgenaam en erflater: Kerkelijke traditie binnen de traditie," in *Traditie en initiatie: Perspectieven voor de toekomst*, ed. Herman Lombaerts and Lieven Boeve, Nike-reeks 36 (Leuven: Acco, 1996), 43–47. See also Lieven Boeve, *Interrupting Tradition: An Essay on Christian Faith in a Postmodern Context* (Leuven/Dudley, MA: Peeters Press, 2003).

4. Herman De Dijn, *Hoe overleven wij de vrijheid? Modernisme, postmodernisme en het mystiek lichaam* (Kapellen: Uitgeverij Pelckmans; Kampen: Kok Agora, 1994), 9.

5. Ibid., 11.

6. For the following section, see Lambert Leijssen, "Sacramentaliteit van de wereld: Meedenken met Georges De Schrijver," in *God ondergronds: Opstellen voor een theologisch vrijdenker. Aangeboden aan professor Georges De Schrijver*, ed. Lieven Boeve and Jacques Haers (Averbode: Altiora, 2001), 317–37, here 329–34.

7. See Lieven Boeve, "Postmodern Sacramento-theology: Retelling the Christian Story," *Ephemerides Theologicae Lovanienses* 74 (1998): 326–43; Jeff Bloechl and Stijn Van den Bossche, "Postmoderniteit, theologie en sacramentologie: Een onderzoeksproject toegelicht," *Jaarboek voor liturgieonderzoek* 13 (1997): 21–48.

8. See the report of this congress: Lieven Boeve and Lambert Leijssen, eds., *Sacramental Presence in a Postmodern Context*, Bibliotheca Ephemeridum Theologicarum Lovaniensium 160 (Leuven: University Press, 2001), with the introduction by Lieven Boeve, "Thinking Sacramental Presence in a Postmodern Context: A Playground for Theological Renewal" (pp. 3–35); and Georges De Schrijver, "Postmodernity and the Withdrawal of the Divine: A Challenge for Theology" (pp. 39–64). I provide a short summary of this article here; see the references to other authors there.

9. Marcel Gauchet, *The Disenchantment of the World: A Political History of Religion*, trans. Oscar Burge (Princeton, NJ: Princeton University Press, 1999).

10. De Schrijver, "Postmodernity and the Withdrawal of the Divine," 59–60, with reference to Jean-Luc Marion, *God Without Being*, trans. Thomas A. Carlson (Chicago: University of Chicago Press, 1991), 10. See also Jean-Luc Marion and John D. Caputo, eds., *Idol and Distance*, trans. Thomas A. Carlson (New York: Fordham University Press, 2001);

Jean-Luc Marion, *Being Given: Toward a Phenomenology of Givenness*, trans. Jeffrey L. Kosky (Stanford: Stanford University Press, 2002).

11. See Stijn Van Den Bossche, "Twee verschillende kijkwijzen: Jean-Luc Marion over idool en icoon," in *God ondergronds*, 339–56.

12. De Schrijver, "Postmodernity and the Withdrawal of the Divine," 62, with reference to Dorothee Sölle, *Mystik und Widerstand "Du stilles Geschrei"* (Hamburg: Piper, 1997), 16.

13. Louis Dupré, "Postmodernity or Late Modernity: Ambiguities in Richard Rorty's Thought," *Metaphysics* 47 (1993): 277–95.

14. Louis Dupré, "The Broken Mirror: The Fragmentation of the Symbolic World," *Stanford Literature Review* 5 (1998): 7–24.

15. Dupré concludes his article "The Broken Mirror" as follows: "We are left with Eliot's 'heap of broken images'. Still the desert of meaning that has produced this glitter cannot afford to dispense with those wobbling beacons. For even these aesthetic symbols with their forever shifting perspectives in an unstable universe yield at least a momentary glimmer of eternity. They are still to be treasured as 'fragments against ruins' (T. S. Eliot, *The Waste Land*)."

16. Marion, *Being Given, Book V: The Gifted*, 248–319.

17. Alexander Schmemann, *The World as Sacrament* (London: Darton, Longman & Todd, 1966). See Mathai Kadavil, "A Journey from East to West: Alexander Schmemann's Contribution to Orthodoxy in the West," *Exchange* 28 (1999): 224–46; idem, *The World as Sacrament: Sacramentality of Creation from the Perspectives of Leonardo Boff, Alexander Schmemann and Saint Ephrem*, Textes et Études Liturgiques/Studies in Liturgy 20 (Leuven: Peeters, 2005).

18. See Byron D. Stuhlman, "The Theme of Creation in the Liturgical Theology of Alexander Schmemann," in *Creation and Liturgy: Studies in Honor of H. Boone Porter*, ed. Ralph McMichael, Jr. (Washington, DC: Pastoral Press, 1993), 113–27.

19. This is the title of the dissertation with which Stijn Van den Bossche, in the framework of the research project, earned his doctorate at the Catholic University of Leuven, Faculty of Theology, on May 27, 2000: *Presentie in differentie: Vier essays over de godsontmoeting in een postmoderne context*.

20. Louis-Marie Chauvet, "The Broken Bread as Theological Figure of Eucharistic Presence," in *Sacramental Presence in a Postmodern Context*, 236–62.

Chapter 5: Sacrament:
The Language of the Self-Giving God

1. D. Power, *Sacrament: The Language of God's Giving* (New York: Crossroad, 1999), 11: "We can write of sacrament as an economy of gift. This lays aside a metaphysical foundation and a subjective foundation to adopt instead an awareness of the Gift that precedes all worldly contours and overflows them...."

2. C. Vos, "Liturgische taal als metaforische taal," in *Nieuwe wegen in de liturgie: De weg van de liturgie—een vervolg*, ed. Marcel Barnard and Nick A. Schuman (Zoetermeer: Meinema, 2002), 93.

Chapter 6: With the Silent Glimmer of God's Spirit

1. See Jan Kerkhofs, SJ, *A Horizon of Kindly Light: A Spirituality for Those with Questions* (London: SCM Press, 1999). This is a beautiful text.

2. See Piet Fransen, "Inwoning Gods en sakramentele genade," in idem, *Hermeneutics of the Councils and Other Studies*, Bibliotheca Ephemeridum Theologicarum Lovaniensium 69 (Leuven: University Press/Peeters, 1985), 393–412.

Chapter 7: Baptism, Confirmation, Eucharist

1. For this section, see Lambert Leijssen, "De kinderdoop en de ene initiatie: Een (post-moderne) sacramentologische reflectie," in *Nieuw leven: Rituelen rond geboorte en doop*, Liturgie in Beweging 1, ed. Gerard Lukken and Jeroen de Wit (Baarn: Gooi en Sticht, 1997), 216–60.

2. See Adelbert Denaux, "De (kinder)doop in de vroege Kerk," in *Levensrituelen: Geboorte en Doopsel*, Kadoc-Studies 20, ed. Lambert Leijssen, Michel Cloet, and Karel Dobbelaere (Leuven: Universitaire Pers Leuven, 1996), 57–69.

3. Lambert Van Dinteren, "De doop in de orthodoxe Kerken," in *Levensrituelen: Geboorte en Doopsel*, 178.

4. Jean-Marie Jaspard, "Geboorte en doopsel vanuit psychofiloso-fische hoek bekeken," in *Levensrituelen: Geboorte en Doopsel*, 45.

5. See Lambert Leijssen, "Het vormsel als sacrament van geloof en als overgangsritueel: Een theologische benadering," in *Levensrituelen: Het Vormsel*, Kadoc-studies 12, ed. Karel Dobbelaere, Lambert Leijssen, and Michel Cloet (Leuven: Universitaire Pers Leuven, 1991), 217–31.

6. Jozef Lamberts, "De doopviering tijdens de Middeleeuwen," in *Levensrituelen: Geboorte en Doopsel*, 71.

7. See Michel Cloet, "Het vormsel in Vlaanderen van ca. 1600 tot ca. 1800: een verwaarloosd sacrament," in *Levensrituelen: Het Vormsel*, 9–23; and Lieve Gevers, "De vormselpraktijk in Vlaanderen in de negentiende en twintigste eeuw: een nieuwe adem?" in *Levensrituelen: Het Vormsel*, 25–46.

8. See Henri Bourgeois, "La place de la confirmation dans l'initiation chrétienne," *Nouvelle Revue Théologique* 115 (1993):516–42, esp. 538–39.

9. Jacques De Visscher, *Een te voltooien leven: Over rituelen van de moderne mens* (Kapellen: Uitgeverij Pelckmans; Kampen: Kok Agora, 1996), 66.

10. Lambert Leijssen, ed., *Confirmation: Origins, History and Pastoral Situation Today*, Textes et Études Liturgiques/Studies in Liturgy 10 (Leuven: Keizersberg Abbey, 1989), 16. See also Lambert Leijssen, "Confirmation in Context," *Louvain Studies* 20 (1995): 294–315, with a report on the pastoral context in the United States as discussed in a summer course at Duquesne University, Pittsburgh, in 1993.

11. Jean-Luc Marion, "Of the Eucharistic Site of Theology," and "The Present and the Gift," in *God Without Being*, trans. Thomas A. Carlson (Chicago/London: University of Chicago Press, 1991), 139–82.

12. Leon Lemmens, *Voor een leven in vriendschap: Eucharistie vanuit Schrift en liturgie*, Verkenningen (Averbode: Altiora, 2000), 104.

13. Ibid., 105.

14. Paul Schruers, *De Kerk als communio*, Verkenningen (Averbode: Altiora, 1999), 74.

15. Ibid., 35.

Chapter 8: Reconciliation and Anointing

1. For this section, see Lambert Leijssen, "Geschiedenis van de christelijke verzoening in vogelvlucht. Hermeneutische reflecties," in

Gebroken bestaan 1: Rituelen rond vergeving en verzoening, Liturgie in Beweging 3, ed. Gerard Lukken and Jeroen de Wit (Baarn: Gooi en Sticht, 1998), 14–33. See the references to the literature there.

2. See Paul De Clerck and Robert Gantoy, "Vers un quatrième régime pénitentiel?" *Communautés et Liturgies* 3 (1983): 191–212.

3. Louis-Marie Chauvet, "Évolutions et révolutions du sacrement de la réconciliation," in *Le Sacrement du pardon entre hier et demain*, Collection Culte et Culture, ed. Louis-Marie Chauvet and Paul De Clerck (Paris: Desclée, 1993), 33–39.

4. Ibid., 39.

5. See Catherine Dooley, "The 1983 Synod of Bishops and the 'Crisis of Confession,'" *Concilium* 23, no. 2 (1987): 18–25.

6. See James Dallen, *The Reconciling Community: The Rite of Penance*, Studies in the Reformed Rites of the Catholic Church 3 (Collegeville, MN: Liturgical Press, 1986); and Joseph A. Favazza, "The Fragile Future of Reconciliation," *Worship* 71 (1997): 236–44.

7. Joseph A. Favazza, "The Efficacy of Ritual Resistance: The Case of Catholic Sacramental Reconciliation," *Worship* 72 (1998): 210–20.

8. Lambert J. Leijssen, "Rahner's Contribution to the Renewal of Sacramentology," *Philosophy & Theology* 9 (1995): 218–19; Herbert Vorgrimler, "La théologie du sacrement de pénitence chez Karl Rahner," *La Maison-Dieu* 214 (1998): 23–29.

9. Jean-Luc Marion, *Being Given: Toward a Phenomenology of Givenness*, trans. Jeffrey L. Kosky (Stanford: Stanford University Press, 2002).

10. Cornelis Verhoeven, "Het alziend oog," *Streven* 65 (1998): 583.

11. For this section, with reference to the literature, see Lambert Leijssen, "De ziekenzalving als sacrament van geloof en 'rite de passage,'" in *Liturgie en kerkopbouw*, ed. Ernest Henau and Frans Jespers (Baarn: Gooi en Sticht, 1993), 127–57.

12. We are leaving the theology of Duns Scotus and the Franciscan school outside of consideration.

13. See also the observations of Jozef Lamberts concerning an "ecclesial liturgy" in his *Geborgen in Zijn liefde: Het sacrament van de ziekenzalving*, Woord en Beleving 14 (Tielt: Lannoo, 1987), 191–95. See also David N. Power, "The Sacrament of the Anointing of the Sick," *Concilium* 27, no. 2 (1991): 84–93.

14. Gisbert Greshake, "Letzte Ölung oder Krankensalbung? Playdoyer für eine differenziertere Theorie und Praxis," *Geist und Leben* 56 (1983): 119–36.

15. Harry Habersma, "Nieuwe vertrouwdheid met de dood," *Streven* 57 (May 1990): 681, with reference to Manu Keirse, "Zingeving in gezondheidszorg," *Praktische Theologie* 12, no. 1 (1985): 26. The fact of one's approaching death is central to the Christian guidelines regarding palliative care, in which Sister Leontine has done groundbreaking work in Saint John's Hospital, Brussels. See Sister Leontine, *Menswaardig sterven* (Leuven: Davidsfonds, 1992). See also Manu Keirse, *Afscheid van moeder: Als sterven een stuk leven wordt* (Tielt: Lannoo, 1992).

Chapter 9: Sacraments of Vocation

1. For this section see Lambert Leijssen and Paul Post, "Huwelijksliturgie: inculturatie van een levensfeest," in *Levensrituelen: Het huwelijk*, Kadoc-studies 24, ed. Roger Burggraeve, Michel Cloet, Karel Dobbelaere, and Lambert Leijssen (Leuven: Universitaire Pers Leuven, 2000), 189–96.

2. See Paul Pas, *De zeven sacramenten op de drempel van het derde millennium*, Nikè-reeks 45 (Leuven: Acco, 1999), 221–23.

3. Erik Borgman, "Een omvattend verbond: De zin van theologische reflectie op het huwelijk," *Tijdschrift voor Theologie* 39 (1999): 107–17, esp. 111.

4. See Louis-Marie Chauvet, *Symbol and Sacrament: A Sacramental Reinterpretation of Christian Existence*, trans. Patrick Madigan and Madeleine Beaumont (Collegeville, MN: Liturgical Press, 1995).

5. Herwi Rikhof, "Waarom maar drie? Een onderzoek naar het sacramenteel merkteken en het huwelijk," in *De lengte en de breedte, de hoogte en de diepte: Peilingen in de theologie van de sacramenten*, ed. Anton H. C. van Eijk and Herwi W. M. Rikhof (Zoetermeer: Meinema, 1996), 98–99.

6. Louis-Marie Chauvet, "Parler du sacrement de mariage aujourd'-hui," in *Pastorale Sacramentelle: Points de repère. Commentaires et guide de travail. I, Les Sacrements de l'initiation chrétienne et le mariage*, Liturgie; Collection de recherche du Centre national de pastoral liturgique 8 (Paris, 1996), 182–205, and an earlier article by the same author: "Le mariage: Un sacrement pas comme les autres," *La Maison-Dieu* 127 (1976): 64–105.

7. See Anton H. C. van Eijk, "Er is meer aan sacramentaliteit," *Tijdschrift voor Liturgie* 83 (1999): 130–43, esp. 135, where he refers to the description of a broader conception of sacramentality in a commentary from the Dutch bishops and theologians: "Every manifestation of salvation in the name of God in the history of individual and social life is sacramental."

8. See Borgman, "Een omvattend verbond," 116: "The union allows room for growth, for different forms in different phases, and it requires creativity in dealing with whatever comes your way. This makes clear that the 'theology of marriage' is a tradition that is open to the present and the future and is established via an extended reflection on whatever happens within the space of the relationship as a union, how people seem to perpetuate this union, to empower it and to enable it to survive." This article by Borgman also appeared in *Rondom Gezin. Driemaandelijks tijdschrift van de interdiocesane Dienst voor Gezinspastoraal* 20 (1999): 129–40.

9. Tijs Michels and Paul Post, "Huwelijk: dynamiek van feest en sacrament," *Tijdschrift voor Liturgie* 81 (1997) 339, with reference to Francisco Taborda, *Sakramente: Praxis und Fest*, Bibliothek Theologie der Befreiung. Die Kirche, Sakrament der Befreiung, trans. Horst Goldstein (Düsseldorf: Patmos, 1988).

10. Michels and Post, "Huwelijk," 341.

11. Borgman, "Een omvattend verbond," 113.

12. Jacques De Visscher, *Een te voltooien leven: Over rituelen van de moderne mens* (Kapellen: Pelckmans; Kampen: Kok Agora, 1996), 122.

13. Ibid., 122, 123.

14. Ibid., 123.

15. Ibid., 134.

16. Liliane Voyé, "Les jeunes et le mariage religieux," *Social Compass* 38 (1991): 405–16.

17. "One is a figure of insignificance if one sees nothing in the ritual but an empty shell, a container without content, a form without foundation and who, supported by the modern prevalence of the rational, tends to condemn the ritual for its emotional and unreflective contents, the lack of technique in its course and the non-empirical aspects that are expected from it" (Liliane Voyé, "Le rite en questions," in *Le rite, source et ressources*, ed. René Devisch, Charles Perrot, Liliane Voyé, and Louis-Marie Chauvet [Brussels: Publications des Facultés Universitaires Saint-Louis, 1995], 105).

18. Louis-Marie Chauvet, *The Sacraments: The Word of God at the Mercy of the Body* (Collegeville, MN: Liturgical Press, 2001), ch. 5, under the subheading "Evangelizing the Rite," and ch. 9, under the subheading "Requests for Sacramental Rites of Passage and Content of Belief."

19. Chauvet, "Parler du sacrement de mariage aujourd'hui," 204: "Let us respect the religious person with his archaisms. It is in that soil that the Word can germinate."

20. Louis-Marie Chauvet, "Le rite et l'éthique: une tension féconde," in *Le rite, source et ressources*, 137, with reference to Paul Ricoeur's reflections on the symbols of evil with the tension between sketches of interiority and exteriority.

21. Lieven Boeve, *Interrupting Tradition: An Essay on Christian Faith in a Postmodern Context*, trans. Brian Doyle (Leuven/Dudley, MA: Peeters, 2003), 115. See ch. 7, "Jesus: Interrupting on Behalf of God."

22. Ibid., 91–96.

23. Ibid., 127.

24. Veerle Draulans and Henk Witte, "Initiatie in de vrij-willigerskerk: Verkenningen in vergelijkend perspectief," in *De kerk in Vlaanderen: avond of dageraad?*, ed. Lieven Boeve (Leuven: Davidsfonds, 1999), 185–88.

25. See Erlinde De Lange and Bert Roebben, "Geloven onder spanning. Sacramentencatechese anno 1999," in *De kerk in Vlaanderen*, 210–28.

26. Ilse Cornu and Stijn Van Den Bossche, "Spirituele beleving van het christelijk huwelijk," in *Levensrituelen: Het Huwelijk*, 248–49.

27. Paul Schruers, *De Kerk als communio*, Verkenningen (Averbode: Altiora, 1999), 30, with reference to Klaus Hemmerle, *Linien des Lebens: Meditationsimpulse zum Johannes-evangelium* (Munich: Neue Stadt, 1996), 69–70.

28. Roger Burggraeve, Michel Cloet, Karel Dobbelaere, and Lambert Leijssen, "Het huwelijk in goede en kwade dagen: Conclusies," in *Levensrituelen: Het huwelijk*, 269–70.

29. For this section see Lambert Leijssen, "De identiteit van de priester na Vaticanum II," *Collationes* 5 (1975): 145–66, with references to the literature there.

30. Walter Kasper, "A New Dogmatic Outlook on the Priestly Ministry," *Concilium* 5, no. 3 (1969): 12–18. See also Hans Küng, "De charismatische structuur van de Kerk," *Concilium* 1, no. 4 (1965): 40–56,

and his book *The Church*, trans. Ray Ockenden and Rosaleen Ockenden (New York: Sheed and Ward, 1967).

31. Karl Rahner, "The Point of Departure in Theology for Determining the Nature of the Priestly Office," in *Theological Investigations*, vol. 12, *Confrontations, 2*, trans. David Bourke (London: Darton, Longman and Todd; New York: Herder and Herder, 1974), 366–72.

32. Edward Schillebeeckx, "Theologische kanttekeningen bij de huidige priester-crisis," *Tijdschrift voor Theologie* 8 (1968): 402–34.

33. On the manner of symbolization see Lambert Leijssen, "De priesterlijke dienst in de kerkgemeenschap," *Collationes* 7 (1977): 131–41.

34. Albert Dondeyne, *Priester en leek* (Antwerpen: Uitgeverij Patmos, 1962), 27–37.

35. Jozef Ratzinger, "Zur Frage nach dem Sinn des priesterlichen Dienstes," *Geist und Leben* 41 (1968): 347–76.

36. Gisbert Greshake, *The Meaning of Christian Priesthood*, trans. Peadar MacSeumais (Dublin: Four Courts Press; Maryland: Christian Classics, 1988), 9.

37. Instead of an epilogue Gisbert Greshake offers "ten principles for a priest's life pattern" by Walter Breuning and Bishop Klaus Hemmerle, the seventh of which reads as follows: "Joint action is more important than isolated action, no matter how imperfect. Thus cooperation in work is more important than work alone, *communio* more important than action" (ibid., 167).

38. Ernest Henau, "Het ambtelijk priesterschap," *Tijdschrift voor Geestelijk Leven* 26 (1970): 637.

Chapter 10: Ecumenical Perspectives

1. For a more detailed treatment of this section, see Lambert Leijssen, "Wat na het BEM-rapport? Liturgisch-sacramentologische reflecties over de haalbaarheid," *Tijdschrift voor Liturgie* 83 (1999): 193–206, with references to the literature. See also Lambert Leijssen, "Oecuménisme, sacrements et postmodernité: Réflections herméneutiques sur la reception du rapport BEM," *Questions Liturgiques/Studies in Liturgy* 81 (2000): 122–38.

2. Jos Vercruysse, *Pelgrims onderweg: Inleiding tot de oecumenische beweging*, Nikè-reeks 41, Publicaties van het Centrum voor Oecumenisch Onderzoek 2 (Leuven: Acco 1998).

3. Johannes Brosseder, "Towards What Unity of the Churches?" *Concilium* 33, no. 3 (1997): 130–38, quotation from 138. Brosseder is chairman of the European community for ecumenical research, *Societas oecumenica*.

4. Ibid., 133.

5. Anton Houtepen, "Volgens de Schriften: De oecumenische beweging op zoek naar nieuwe methoden," in *Een werkzame dialoog: Oecumenische bijdragen over de kerk 30 jaar na Vaticanum II*, Nikè-reeks 38, Publicaties van het Centrum voor Oecumenisch Onderzoek 1, ed. Robrecht Michiels and Jacques Haers (Leuven: Acco 1997), 17–39.

6. Ibid., 29.

7. Ibid.

8. Jean-Luc Marion, *God Without Being*, trans. Thomas A. Carlson (Chicago/London: University of Chicago Press, 1991). Original: first edition, *Dieu sans l'être* (Paris: Librairie Arthème Fayard, 1982; second edition, Paris: Quadrige/Presses Universitaires de France, 1991).

9. Jean-Luc Marion, *Being Given: Toward a Phenomenology of Givenness*, trans. Jeffrey L. Kosky (Stanford: Stanford University Press, 2002). Original: *Étant donné: Essai d'une phénoménologie de la donation*, Épiméthée (Paris: Presses Universitaires de France, 1997).

10. Louis-Marie Chauvet, *The Sacraments: The Word of God at the Mercy of the Body* (Collegeville, MN: Liturgical Press, 2001). Original: *Les sacraments: Parole de Dieu au risque du corps*, Recherches (Paris: Les Éditions de l'Atelier/Les Éditions Ouvrières, 1997).

11. Martien Brinkman, "Aspecten van een gemeenschappelijk sacramentsbegrip," in *Een werkzame dialoog*, 71.

12. Johann Reikerstorfer, "The God of Christians and the Fragmentation of the Postmodern World," *Concilium* 33, no. 3 (1997): 16.

13. J. N. Collins, *Diakonia: Re-interpreting the Ancient Sources* (Oxford: Oxford University Press, 1990); idem, *Are All Christians Ministers?* (Collegeville, MN: Liturgical Press, 1992).

14. Henk Witte, "Oecumene als interkerkelijk communicatief proces," in *Een werkzame dialoog*, 100–101.

15. Reikerstorfer, "God of Christians," 31.

STUDY QUESTIONS

Chapter 1: Life Rituals:
Metaphoric Celebrations of Existence

1. The human person is by nature a *homo religiosus* who expresses a relation to the divine through rituals. What are some of the life events that human beings since time immemorial have sought to "consecrate" through ritual?

2. The German author Goethe states, "That which [the human person] should love and do, he cannot think of alone and isolated....The sacraments are the high point of a religion, the visible symbol of an extraordinary divine favour and grace." Discuss this in relation to one or all of the seven Christian sacraments.

3. Why do non-churchgoers still ask for sacraments (and Christian burial) at crucial life moments? In this connection, what are the pastoral implications for the author's statement, "Christian sacraments are surely not to be reduced to mere rites of passage"?

Chapter 2: New Visions in Sacramental Theology

1. Name some instances in which one or more of the seven Christian sacraments stand in danger of being reduced to "vending machines" of grace.

2. What does Edward Schillebeeckx mean when he describes the sacraments as "encounters with a person"?

3. How does Karl Rahner's concept of "sacrament" exemplify the statement that "Contemporary theology is about discovering God's salvation-in-the-world"?

4. What are the advantages of the celebrational model of the sacraments? Can you see any risks?

Chapter 3: The Seven Sacraments

1. Very briefly, in what specific way does each of the seven sacraments touch one of the "important moments of Christian life"?

Chapter 4: Sacramental Presence in a Postmodern Context

1. "The space of emptiness and distance is the place to find God again." Discuss this statement.

2. If we see the world as God's gift, in which God "gives himself to us and opens himself in self-emptying," what implications does this have for sacramental theology?

3. What significance does the Emmaus story have in the sacramental theology of Louis-Marie Chauvet?

Chapter 5: Sacrament: The Language of the Self-Giving God

1. Discuss the distinction between "icon" and "idol" in relation to sacramental theology.

2. "There is an entire gamut of extraverbal communication in liturgical celebrations." Name some instances connected with one or more of the sacraments.

3. What does it mean to say that "liturgy speaks about and to the Invisible"?

Chapter 6: With the Silent Glimmer of God's Spirit

1. In classical theology, what is the difference between uncreated grace and created grace? In a renewed understanding, how can we conceive of created grace?

2. Draw out the implications of thinking of the Holy Spirit's activity as light. What does this mean for the sacraments?

3. How does Rahner's distinction between prevenient grace and accepted grace help to clarify postmodern thinking of the sacraments in terms of gift?

Chapter 7: Baptism, Confirmation, Eucharist: Sacraments of Christian Initiation

1. With what four motives does Adelbert Denaux clarify the meaning of early Christian baptism?

2. How did the early church regard infant baptism? What is the place of infant baptism in postmodern thought?

3. Briefly describe the development of confirmation as a separate sacrament of initiation.

4. How can we think of confirmation in a postmodern context?

5. Describe the classical way of explaining the real presence of Christ in the Eucharist.

6. How can we speak of the Eucharist in postmodern terms?

Chapter 8: Reconciliation and Anointing: Sacraments of Healing

1. Describe the three historical ways of thinking of the sacrament of penance up until the Second Vatican Council. Who were some of the theologians who contributed to the development of the theology of this sacrament?

2. What are some of the challenges and considerations in formulating a postmodern theology of and approach to the sacrament of reconciliation?

3. Describe the history of the anointing of the sick as it developed from New Testament times.

4. What changes in our approach to the anointing of the sick have been brought about since Vatican II? What arguments can be offered in favor of someone other than a priest being the minister of this sacrament?

Chapter 9: Sacraments of Vocation: Marriage and Holy Orders

1. Discuss the characterization of Christian marriage as a "festival of life." Why can we not label the marriage ceremony as a "magic ritual of making an oath"?

2. Discuss some possible pastoral approaches to ensuring that church weddings are not reduced to meaningless ritual or external pomp by those who lack a life commitment to the church. How can the request for a church marriage be utilized as a "teaching moment"?

3. Name some of the causes of the current crisis in the priesthood. What role does the anti-institutional tendency of postmodernism play?

4. Name some of the outstanding features of the Second Vatican Council's contribution to the concept of the priesthood.

Chapter 10: Ecumenical Perspectives

1. Name some of the ways in which other churches can agree with the postmodern view of the sacraments as dynamic gifts of the Spirit and the language of the self-giving God.

2. How will unity among the churches eventually be realized? What image does theologian Jos Vercruysse offer for this process?

3. What models do such theologians as Johann Reikerstorfer and Henk Witte offer for the future of the ecumenical movement?